BETTER
WRITING ▶
RIGHT NOW!

Using Words
to Your Advantage

Francine D. Galko

LEARNINGEXPRESS

NEW YORK

Library of Congress Cataloging-in-Publication Data:
Galko, Francine.
   Better writing right now : using words to your advantage / by Francine Galko.—1st ed.
     p.   cm.
   ISBN 1-57685-402-7
   1. English language—Rhetoric. 2. Report writing. 3. Business writing. I. Title.

PE1408 .G25 2002
808'.042—dc21   2001050784

ISBN 1-57685-402-7

Printed in the United States of America
9 8 7 6 5 4 3 2 1
First Edition

For more information or to place an order, contact LearningExpress at:
   900 Broadway
   Suite 604
   New York, NY 10003

Or visit us at:
   www.learnatest.com

ABOUT THE AUTHOR

Francine D. Galko is currently a freelance writer, editor, and project manager. She has edited pre-GED and GED math preparation work texts, and has also written a basic math and algebra study guide with practice materials and interactive CD-ROMs. In addition, Ms. Galko has written and edited other science, language arts, ESL, EFL, and instructional materials. She currently resides in Dallas, Texas.

Contents

Introduction ▶

Let's say you're at the bookstore and you're trying to decide whether or not to buy this book. You wonder: Will it really help me write better? Is it any different from the other books on the shelf? How can this book improve my writing? If these are some of the questions you have, then read on—you'll find the answers here!

Better Writing Right Now is a step-by-step guide to writing. It takes you from the blank page and walks you through the steps of the writing process so that you can conquer any school writing assignment—including timed essay exams and research papers. It also provides tips and formats you can use for writing resumes, cover letters, general business letters, memos, e-mails, and reports for work. Along the way, you'll learn basic writing skills, and you'll gain the confidence you need to succeed in any situation that requires you to write.

This book gives you more than the information you need to become a better writer. It also gives you example after example of strategies that work and provides opportunities to practice those strategies. Take advantage of each practice, because here you can safely experiment with techniques and develop expert skills before you have to use them for class, work, or correspondence. Your work in this book can be for your eyes only—so stretch your fingers, stretch your imagination, and don't be afraid to see your writing take shape.

▶ Is This Book for You?

This book was written to help anyone who wants to work on writing skills. If you know very little about writing or you're just not confident when you get a writing assignment at school, this book is the first step to good writing. If you already have a good command of the language, but need some reference points for your writing, or if you're just interested in fine-tuning your writing skills, this book acts as a comprehensive guide for writers. So if you are ready to improve your writing skills—this book is for you!

► How This Book Is Organized

This book is organized into short lessons. Each of the first twelve lessons focuses on one step in the writing process. You begin by learning how to read and understand a writing assignment and then how to develop a topic. The first lessons take you step-by-step through the process of completing any writing assignment. Concluding lessons in this book teach you how to deal with special writing situations—such as timed essay exams, research papers, resumes, cover letters, and other business correspondence.

Each lesson gives you step-by-step information for tackling every kind of writing problem—from writer's block to basic writing mechanics. You'll also find annotated examples of good and poor writing samples and ways you can tell them apart. Then, you're given a chance to practice what you've learned. Answers to the practice sets are provided at the back of the book, so you can check your work as you go along.

As you work through this book, you'll notice that the lessons are sprinkled with all kinds of helpful tips and icons. Look for these icons and the tips they provide.

Writing Tip   When you see this icon, you know that practical writing information follows. Many of the writing tips include additional strategies or well-organized reference information that you can return to time and time again.

Test Taking Tip   This icon gives you tips for taking writing tests. Look for these if you are preparing for an essay test or a test that involves open-ended or free-response questions.

Think About It   Extra information and more in-depth discussions are marked with this icon.

► How Is This Book Different from Other Writing Books?

Take a minute to flip through the pages of this book. Then, flip through the pages of another writing book you are considering. See something different?

First off, this book shows you how to conquer writer's block. It provides numerous approaches to writing that you won't find in other books. There's a whole lesson on using graphic organizers—not just charts and tables—to organize your ideas. If you are comfortable with conventional approaches to writing, they're here, too. And this book can be a resource for you long after you've become a confident and proficient writer!

Better Writing Right Now! is a hands-on guide to writing. Unlike many of the other writing books out there, this one involves *you*. It walks you through any writing assignment you might have—from writing an essay for class to writing a memo for your boss.

Moreover, this book doesn't just *tell* you how to write better. It *shows* you how to write better. You'll find page after page of examples of strategies that work. They're not just described—you actually see them in action. You'll also find examples of real writing with callouts that show you the strategies and steps behind the finished product—this way you can see the writing process at work.

Writing is a lifelong skill that you will use in school, at work, and in your personal life. With this book, you'll become a more proficient and confident writer. So, go ahead, write better right now!

Deciding What to Say—
Preparing to Write

Getting Started

LESSON SUMMARY

Have you ever been given a writing assignment and felt lost? Are you unsure of how to approach a writing assignment? Then, you're in the right place! This lesson will show you how to get started. You'll learn how to interpret the direction words or questions in different types of writing assignments.

So you've been given a writing assignment, and you aren't quite sure how to begin. First, you aren't sure what to say. And second, you don't know how to say it. Here's how to get started.

▶ UNDERSTANDING DIFFERENT TYPES OF WRITING ASSIGNMENTS

The first step is reading and understanding your writing assignment. Read your assignment carefully. Then, reread your assignment, asking yourself these questions.

- What is my topic?
- How much am I expected to write? How long should my finished paper be?
- Who is my audience?
- How long will I have to complete the assignment?
- What is the *main* purpose of the assignment? Is it to show that I learned the material for a particular class, to analyze a piece of literature or situation, or to showcase my writing ability?

Some writing assignments give you a question or a topic on which to write. Others are more open-ended and you have to come up with a topic or question that you will address in your writing. What do these different kinds of writing assignments look like? Here are some samples.

When the Topic Is Provided. When a topic is given, your writing assignment might look like these examples. These are the types of writing assignments you will often find on standardized tests and other timed exercises. You are also likely to find these types of exercises in your non-English classes. It's typical for humanities, science, and social science classes to expect you to write about the material you have covered in class.

- Write a letter to the editor of your local newspaper explaining your point of view on year-round schools.
- Your state is considering building a prison in your community. How do you feel about having a prison near your home?
- Is it a good idea for schools to incorporate technology in the classroom? Why or why not?
- Nuclear energy avoids the mining and pollution problems of traditional fossil fuels, but it also poses contamination and health risks. Do you think governments should build nuclear power plants? State your opinion and support it with convincing reasons.
- Explain how your local recycling program works.
- How did the Korean War differ from the Vietnam War? What were the causes and results of each war?
- Compare the goals and achievements of the French Revolution with those of the American Revolution.
- Identify three main causes of disease. What are two causes of infectious diseases? Give an example of a disease caused by each factor you discuss.

When a Topic Is Not Provided. When you are expected to develop your own topic, your writing assignment will be open-ended as the following examples are. Usually you will be given more time to complete these types of writing assignments, and you will often find them in English and composition classes. These types of questions are also common on school application forms.

- What would you do if you were President for one day?
- Write an essay about a childhood memory.
- Describe your ideal partner in life.
- Write a five-page research paper about a subject that interests you.
- Write an essay giving advice on a topic you are familiar with.
- Describe a social problem in your community and suggest ways to address it.
- What are your three greatest accomplishments?
- Write an editorial on an issue about which you have strong feelings.
- Describe a specific work of art and discuss how it makes you feel.

▶ BREAKING DOWN THE ASSIGNMENT WHEN A TOPIC IS GIVEN

Often the assignment will tell you exactly what is wanted in the essay. You just have to identify the key words and provide the information requested. Use the direction words to guide your writing. What are direction words? They include words, such as *describe, explain, discuss, compare*—you've probably seen them in lots of writing assignments.

Example: *Explain how your local recycling program works. Trace the movement of cans, jars, and newspapers from your home to the point where they are recycled. Give examples of products that can be made from the materials you put in your recycle bin at home.*

SUBJECT	DIRECTIONS
how your local recycling program works	Explain
the movement of cans, jars, and newspapers from your home to the point where they are recycled	Trace
of products that can be made from the materials you put in your recycle bin at home	Give examples

Example: Assume that you have just completed a unit in your biology class on genetics, and your biology teacher has given you the following writing assignment. Break the writing assignment into its subject and direction words. (Don't panic if you don't know the answer to this question. Unless you're studying genetics right now in another class, you're not supposed to know the answer!)

Describe gene therapy. Explain how it has been used to treat cystic fibrosis. Discuss why gene therapy is not yet considered a cure for cystic fibrosis.

SUBJECT	DIRECTIONS
gene therapy	Describe
how gene therapy has been used to treat cystic fibrosis	Explain
why gene therapy is yet not considered a cure for cystic fibrosis	Discuss

PRACTICE

Assume that you have just covered the material requested in each of the following writing assignments. Remember, your task is only to break each writing assignment into its subject and direction words. (Don't worry if you don't know the answers to these questions.) Check your response against the answer key at the back of the book.

1. Identify the vectors involved in the transmission of rabies from dogs to humans, and describe three ways to prevent the spread of rabies.

_____

_____

_____

_____

2. Discuss the implications of the argument that behaving ethically makes good business sense. Relate this argument to the behavior of companies today.

_____

_____

_____

_____

3. Compare western European culture with Islamic culture during the Middle Ages. Include information about each culture's scientific accomplishments, literature, and concepts of law and justice.

_____

_____

_____

_____

4. Review the reasons that the U. S. government decided to build a canal across the Isthmus of Panama.

_____

_____

_____

_____

5. Identify four factors that affect the rate of photosynthesis and explain the effect of each factor on the rate of photosynthesis.

_____

_____

_____

_____

TEST TAKING TIP

WRITING ASSIGNMENTS ARE written in their own language. If you know how to interpret the language, you will usually know how you should respond. Look for these direction words as you read your assignments.

WHEN YOU SEE THIS WORD	YOU WILL NEED TO
Analyze	separate the subject into different parts and discuss each part
Argue	give your opinion on a topic and support it with examples, facts, or other details
Assess	tell what is good and bad about a given topic and explain how you arrived at your conclusions
Classify	organize the subject into groups and discuss the logic behind your grouping
Compare	point out how the items are alike and different
Contrast	point out how the items are different
Define	give meaning to the term
Describe	tell what the subject is like
Discuss	list the main parts or issues of the subject and elaborate on each one
Evaluate	tell what is good and bad about a given topic and explain how you arrived at your conclusions
Explain	support your statements with specific facts, examples, and so on; elaborate on the logic you used to make your conclusions
Give evidence	back up your statements with facts, examples, or other supporting information
Give examples	use specific details, facts, or situations to make your point
Identify	name or list the items requested
Illustrate	give specific examples
Include	put this information in the essay
Indicate	tell what you think about a subject and how you arrived at your conclusion
List	name the items requested
Outline	organize the main points of the subject
Relate	point out the connections between the items indicated
Review	list and discuss the main points of the subject
Summarize	briefly describe the main points of the topic
Support	give evidence to back up your statements
Trace	list and describe the points or events in a logical or chronological order

Many assignments will not include direction words. Instead, these assignments will be worded as a question. Questions without direction words require you to figure out what information is wanted.

Example: Translate the writing assignment into its subject and direction words.

How are aerobic exercise and resistance exercise alike and different? How does each kind of exercise affect the body? What are some examples of each type of exercise?

SUBJECT	DIRECTIONS
aerobic exercise and resistance exercise	Compare and contrast
how each kind of exercise affects the body	Explain
of types of aerobic exercises and anaerobic exercises	Give examples

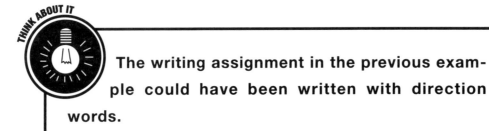

THINK ABOUT IT

The writing assignment in the previous example could have been written with direction words.

Compare and contrast aerobic exercise with resistance exercise. Explain how each kind of exercise affects the body. Give examples of each type of exercise.

Get in the habit of interpreting your writing assignments in this way. Here are some examples of writing assignments you are likely to see in your other classes. Don't worry if you can't answer these questions right now. They are intended for a student who has just covered the requested material in class. You aren't supposed to know the answers to these questions. Just focus on how each question is worded with and without direction words.

AS A QUESTION	WITH DIRECTION WORDS
How does your local recycling program work? What path do the cans, jars, and newspapers take from your home to the point where they are recycled? What are some examples of products that can be made from the materials you put in your recycle bin at home?	Explain how your local recycling program works. Trace the movement of cans, jars, and newspapers from your home to the point where they are recycled. Give examples of products that can be made from the materials you put in your recycle bin at home.
How is international financial management similar to domestic financial management?	Compare international financial management with domestic financial management.
What are multinational corporations? What economic roles do they play?	Define the term *multinational corporation*. Identify the economic roles that multinational corporations play.
What is gene therapy? How has gene therapy been used to treat cystic fibrosis? Why is gene therapy not yet considered a cure for cystic fibrosis?	Describe gene therapy. Explain how it has been used to treat cystic fibrosis. Discuss why gene therapy is not yet considered a cure for cystic fibrosis.
How did the Korean War differ from the Vietnam War? What were the causes and results of each war?	Contrast the Korean War with the Vietnam War. Identify the causes and results of each war.

PRACTICE ▶

Translate each writing assignment into its subject and direction words. Keep in mind that you aren't supposed to know the answers to these questions. Just focus on how each question is worded and how those words translate into direction words. Check your answers against the answer key at the back of the book.

6. What are your goals in life? How do you plan to reach your goals?

_____
_____
_____
_____

7. What are the three main tasks of marketing?

_____
_____
_____
_____

8. How does the representation of courage differ in *Henry V* and in *The Charge of the Light Brigade*?

_____
_____
_____
_____

9. How does economic imperialism differ from political imperialism?

_____
_____
_____
_____

10. What were the foreign policy objectives of Italy, Germany, and Japan in the 1930s? How did each nation achieve its objectives?

_____
_____
_____
_____

Choosing Your Own Topic

LESSON SUMMARY

In the last lesson, you learned how to take apart writing assignments that had very specific topics. But what if your assignment doesn't give you a topic to begin with? What if the topic is left wide open? This lesson will give you some strategies for choosing a topic if one is not provided for you in the writing assignment. It will also show you how to determine if your topic is appropriate for your assignment.

O ften a writing assignment will not be as specific as the ones you have been working with in the last lesson. Instead, the assignment will be open ended. Here are some techniques you can use to find your own topic when you are given an open-ended writing assignment:

- Explore your own areas of expertise.
- Browse different sources for ideas.
- Keep a clip file.
- Write in a journal.
- Ask others for ideas.
- Glean ideas from all around you.

Let's look at how you might go about using each of these techniques.

Exploring your own areas of expertise. Everyone has unique interests and areas of expertise. You may find that you are already interested in or knowledgeable about a topic that you can expand into a topic to fit a particular writing assignment. These questions may help you identify an appropriate topic.

- What are your hobbies? What clubs have you participated in?
- What types of jobs have you had in the past or what type of career are you interested in pursuing?
- What types of volunteer or community service projects have you participated in?
- What places have you visited or would you like to visit?
- What pets do you have or would you like to have one day?

Browsing different sources for ideas. Browse through an encyclopedia, magazine, book of quotations, or surf the Internet. You might find a topic that interests you and fits your writing assignment, but don't copy the information! You can use it as a starting point for your own work, though.

Keeping a clip file. We all have ideas that we do not have time to pursue. You might start a folder or notebook of ideas that you can set aside for future reference. Photocopy or clip articles or tidbits that interest you as you come across them and place them in your clip file. When you need a writing topic, you can go to your clip file for ideas.

Writing in a journal. Like a clip file, a journal can be a place where you keep ideas you can come back to later. You can use your journal to record your observations and reflections as well as quotations from other sources. If something unusual happens, you can describe the incident and your feelings about it in your journal. What was special about this event? If you overhear someone say something that impresses you, you can write it down in your journal and describe your feelings about it. Use your journal to help you explore your thoughts and to make connections to your life. Then, when you are looking for a topic to write about, you can go back and reread your journal entries.

Asking others for ideas. Your friends, family, classmates, and coworkers are also good sources of ideas that fit a writing assignment. Talking to others can help you get a better idea of what you think. It can also help you explore what you want to say in your writing.

Gleaning ideas from your environment. Pay attention to everything around you. You will be surprised how many sources for ideas you already have. Here are a few more suggestions.

- radio, television, the Internet
- films
- music
- visual art
- your dreams
- your memories and personal experiences
- conversations with your friends and family
- literature
- your imagination

- your personal interests
- magazines, newspapers, periodicals, CD-ROMs
- research

Check your answers against the answer key at the back of the book.

1. Choose one of the following topics. Then, write a journal entry for 15–20 minutes. If you need more space than is provided below, use the blank pages at the end of this book.
   a. Think about something unusual that you witnessed recently. What happened? What was unusual about the experience? What about this experience struck you? How did you feel coming away from the experience?
   b. Make a list of things you are interested in or know a lot about. Then choose one of the topics and write about it. Describe the interest. How did you become knowledgeable about it? Why does it interest you? What does this interest say about you?

2. List a few good sources for the topic ideas in the following writing assignments.

   a. Describe a social problem in your community, and suggest ways to address it.

   _____

   _____

   _____

   _____

   b. Describe a specific work of art and discuss how it makes you feel.

   _____

   _____

   _____

   _____

   c. What are your three greatest accomplishments?

   _____

   _____

   _____

   _____

3. Use one of the techniques described in this lesson to come up with your own topic for each of the following writing assignments. If you need more space than is provided below, use the blank pages at the end of this book. Remember, you only need to list topics.

   a. Write a five-page research paper about a subject that interests you.

   _____

   _____

   _____

   _____

   _____

   _____

   _____

   _____

   _____

   _____

   _____

   b. Write a two-page essay giving advice on a topic with which you are familiar.

   _____

   _____

   _____

   _____

   _____

   _____

   _____

   _____

   _____

   _____

   _____

   _____

▶ EVALUATING YOUR TOPIC IDEAS

You will probably generate a number of interesting ideas to write about, but not all of your ideas will be a perfect fit for the assignment. When choosing which topic to write about, remember that your topic should

- work with the length of the writing assignment you've been given.
- be interesting to you.
- meet the purpose of the writing assignment.
- be appropriate for your audience.
- be appropriate for the form of your writing.

Let's briefly discuss each of the characteristics of an appropriate topic.

Choose a topic that is appropriate to the length specified. Usually, your writing assignment will give you an idea of how much you are expected to write. Sometimes, you will be given a page range, such as 1–2 pages, or a word count, such as 500 words. If your writing assignment is to write a paragraph, don't choose a topic that requires 10 pages to introduce. Your topic should be narrow enough to fit into the given length, yet broad enough for you to be able to write about it.

Choose a topic that you are interested in. If you are truly interested in your topic, your enthusiasm will show in your writing. You will be more likely to present the information in a way that interests your reader, and you will enjoy the writing more. Just because you are interested in a topic doesn't mean that you are an expert on it, but you can do research to find out what you need to know.

Choose a topic that meets the purpose of the writing assignment. People write for different reasons and writing assignments have different purposes. Identify the purpose of the writing assignment or establish a purpose for your writing. Your purpose might be to inform, persuade, or entertain your audience. It might be to tell a story or simply to express yourself. Make sure that your topic fits your purpose. Use these questions to help you set a purpose for your writing.

- What is the purpose of the writing assignment? Why was this assignment given to me?
- What do I want to accomplish in this piece of writing?
- What response do I want to get from my audience?

Choose a topic that is appropriate for your audience. Imagine your audience. Would they be interested in how you restore a '57 Chevy? If the audience is the College Placement Board, they just might like to know that you have the skills, organization, and drive to tackle such a project. Besides, there's plenty to tell because it's *your* story. Who are you writing for? For your teacher, your boss, your classmates, a college admissions officer, or simply a general audience? Knowing who your audience is can help you choose what you will say and how you will say it. If you are writing about training your dog for your kennel club, your approach will be different than if you are writing about training your dog for your school newspaper. Although you don't have to identify your audience before you start writing, it can sometimes be helpful in ruling out inappropriate topics. For example, you might not want to write about a very technical or specialized topic for an audience that is not knowledgeable in that field—unless you will be able to simplify the information without losing the meaning and interest level of the topic. Moreover, you might not want to write about a very personal topic for an audience that might not be sensitive to your feelings. Once you know who your audience is, you can use these questions to guide your writing.

- What will my audience find most interesting about this topic?
- What does my audience already know about this topic?
- What parts of this topic will be hard to explain or will require technical terms?
- Why is my audience reading this piece of writing?

Choose a topic that is appropriate for the form of your writing. Your writing can take on many different forms. It might be a poem, a report, an essay, a newspaper article, a letter, a story, a play, or even a speech. Sometimes the form of your writing may be stated in the writing assignment, but other times you will be free to choose your own form. If your writing assignment specifies a form, make sure that your topic is appropriate.

PRACTICE ▶

Check your answers against the answer key at the back of the book.

4. For each writing assignment described below, tell who the audience is and for what they would be looking in your writing.

   a. an essay on a college application form

_____

_____

_____

_____

   b. a letter to the editor of your local newspaper

_____

_____

_____

_____

   c. an essay on a biology test

_____

_____

_____

_____

   d. a research paper for a college composition class

_____

_____

_____

5. Choose a piece of writing. The writing can be from any source. Then, answer the following questions about the writing.

a. What is the topic?

_____

_____

b. How long is the piece of writing?

_____

c. What is the purpose of the writing?

_____

_____

_____

_____

d. Who is the main audience?

_____

_____

e. What is the form of the writing?

_____

f. Did the writer achieve his or her goals? Give specific examples to support your opinion.

_____

_____

_____

_____

_____

_____

LESSON

Using Prewriting Strategies

LESSON SUMMARY

Still not really sure about what to write? This lesson will show you how to explore your topic and ways to write about it. Even if you think you know exactly what you want to write, this lesson can help you be more confident and creative about what you want to say. It will give you many strategies for coming up with the information you will need to begin writing.

Now that you have decided on a topic, you are ready to begin exploring what you want to say about the topic and how you will say it. There are a number of techniques to explore ideas about your topic and different ways to approach your writing.

▶ EXPLORING YOUR IDEAS

Here are some strategies you can use to develop your topic.

- **Brainstorming**—let your ideas flow without judging them
- **Freewriting**—write down your thoughts as they come to you
- **Asking questions**—make a list of questions about your topic
- **Mapping** (also called clustering or webbing)—make a visual diagram of your ideas about a topic
- **Journaling**—write your thoughts in a journal
- **Listing**—make a list of your ideas about a topic

- **Visualizing** (also called image streaming)—imagine yourself in another situation and describe the situation from your point of view
- **Using charts**—group your ideas visually in charts or tables

Use the examples and activities below to practice some to these techniques.

▶ BRAINSTORMING

Brainstorming is a way to come up with ideas either alone or in a group. The main principle behind brainstorming is to let your ideas flow without judging them. First, you generate the ideas. Later, you can come back to them and toss out the ones that won't work. One way to brainstorm is to begin with a word or phrase and let your ideas flow for a set time. Jot down whatever comes to your mind during the brainstorming period. In a group, you might freely suggest ideas as they come to mind. Elect one person to record the ideas of the group. Use your brainstorming to develop the topic or to come up with more examples and details.

Example: This student wanted to write a descriptive paragraph about her father. After brainstorming, she placed a checkmark beside the items she plans to use in her paragraph.

- ✔ Tall
- ✔ Balding
- ✔ Slim
- Wise
- ✔ Loud
- ✔ Authoritative
- Determined
- ✔ Usually wears a suit
- ✔ Warm, friendly laugh
- Good advice usually
- Conservative
- Strong
- Busy
- ✔ Drums fingers

Before brainstorming, the writer felt like there was nothing much to say about her father. Now she has some ideas to work with, because she has a number of details she can use to describe her father's appearance. There are many different ways she can use this information in her paragraph. For example, she could group the characteristics as types or examples of her father's appearance. She could even pick out one or two of the most important characteristics and brainstorm anecdotes that demonstrate these characteristics.

Check your answers against the answer key at the back of the book.

   1. Choose one of the following topics. Then, brainstorm either alone or in a small group for 10–15 minutes as you list ideas that could be included in a writing assignment.
      a. the Internet
      b. pets
      c. education
      d. travel

_____
_____
_____
_____
_____
_____
_____
_____
_____
_____
_____
_____
_____
_____
_____
_____
_____
_____
_____
_____

▶ FREEWRITING

Like brainstorming, freewriting is writing down your thoughts as they come to you. When freewriting, you let your sentences flow freely without thinking about whether the ideas are appropriate or the grammar is perfect. You just start writing. Write quickly and try not to stop. Usually, you freewrite on a topic for a set period of time or number of pages without rereading or correcting what you have written. You can freewrite with pen and paper or on the computer—do whichever comes more naturally to you. People often freewrite when they keep a journal. It's also a good way to generate ideas for a topic. When you finish freewriting, read what you have written and check off the most interesting facts or ideas to use later.

Example: This student wanted to write a paragraph about a travel experience. Of course it needs revision, but there are many good ideas upon which to build.

> I was very surprised by how many farms we saw when we landed. The next thing that impressed me most was the lack of people in such a large airport. This changed when we got to the airport exit which was jam-packed with people. The schedule board made a nice clicking noise. On the bus ride in we saw many billboards and it took 1 hour to get to the city. Check in at the dormitory was easy and we unpacked. Next we went on a hunt for food as it was Sunday evening. We found an open kiosk and bought some peanuts and soda. Then back home to the dorm at 2 AM. The next day we immediately went to Red Square and checked out the Kremlin and St. Basil's. The department store GUM had a surprising selection of items. Paying $1 to go to the fancy French stores was quite a shock. We had pizza for lunch.

PRACTICE ▶

Check your answers against the answer key at the back of the book.

2. Choose one of the following topics. Then, freewrite for 5–10 minutes.
   a. a time you got lost
   b. a visit from a friend
   c. a first day at school
   d. a day at work

_____
_____
_____
_____
_____
_____
_____
_____
_____
_____
_____
_____
_____
_____
_____
_____
_____

► ASKING QUESTIONS

Asking questions about your topic is another way to help you generate ways to approach your topic. There are different ways of using this technique. You might start by listing the following question words on a piece of paper and by answering them individually.

WH-questions
Who
What
When
Where
Why
How

Another approach is to take a poll—ask others WH-questions about your topic.

Example: When given the following writing assignment, this student made a long list of WH-questions about the topic.

Is it a good idea for schools to incorporate technology in the classroom? Why or why not?

Who would be affected by technology in the classroom?
Who will pay for it?
Who will get to use it?
Who will benefit from it?
What technology will be used?
What will be taught using technology?
What limitations are there?
When will it be used?
When can teachers use it?
Who will teach teachers how to use it?
Where will the technology be kept? In each classroom?
Who will maintain it?
Why do students need this?
Why is technology important?
How will the technology be used?
How will costs be kept low?
How much technology are we talking about?
What's wrong with schools the way they are now?
What happens when the existing technology becomes obsolete?
What is technology?
What if schools don't have technology?

Although all of these questions are not relevant to the writing assignment, the student has come up with many interesting ways of tackling the writing assignment.

Check your answers against the answer key at the back of the book.

3. Ask questions to generate ideas about the following topic.
The genes in genetically modified foods have been manipulated in some way and usually contain genes from a different kind of life-form mixed with their own genes. Should food manufacturers be required to label genetically modified foods? Why or why not?

_____
_____
_____
_____
_____
_____
_____
_____
_____
_____
_____
_____
_____
_____

▶ MAPPING

Mapping is also called clustering or webbing. When you map your ideas, you make a visual diagram about a topic. Often the topic is circled in the center of a page. From there, the writer draws spokes linking ideas together. Mapping helps you generate new ideas and relate them to one another. A map can be very simple or more involved like the one on the next page.

Example: This writer used mapping to explore his ideas about legalizing drugs when given the following writing assignment.

Should drugs be legalized in the United States? Why or why not?

The writer generates a number of different ideas and approaches when looking at the issue of drugs and the consequences of legalizing them in this country.

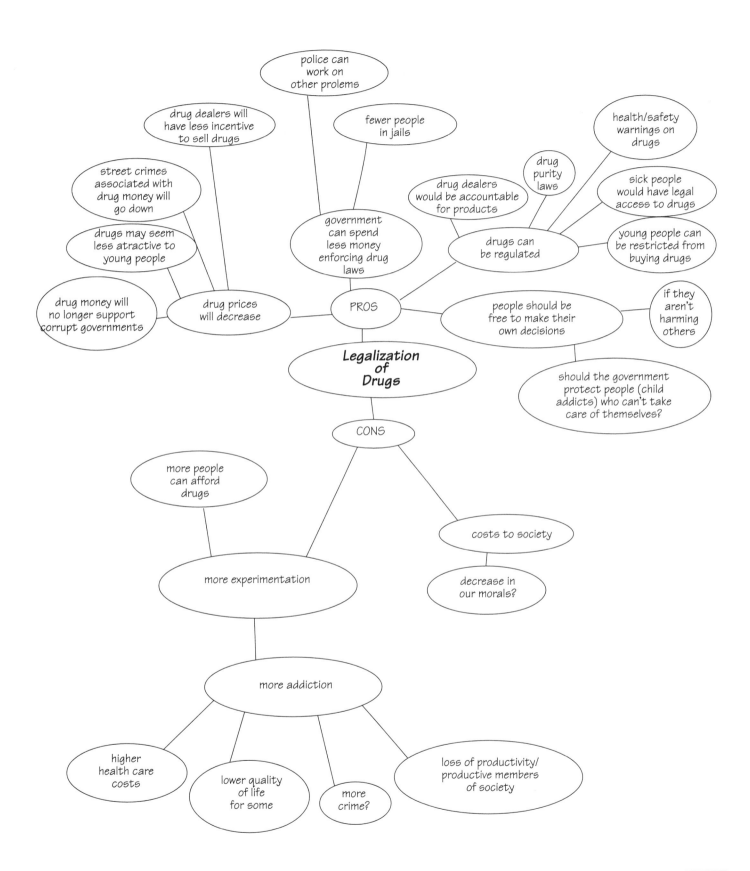

Check your answers against the answer key at the back of the book.

4. Use mapping to generate ideas about the following topic.
Each of us has unique abilities, aptitudes, or personality traits that makes us special in some way. What makes you special?

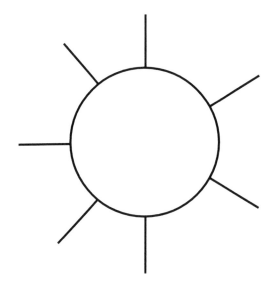

▶ LISTING

When you list, you make a column of words or phrases.

Example: Assume you are given this writing assignment.

Describe a social problem in your community and suggest ways to address it.

You might start by listing all the problems you've read about or heard in the news lately. Here's one possible list.

- Animal rights
- Violence in schools
- Poverty
- Hunger
- Crime
- Unemployment
- Teenage pregnancy
- Lack of universal healthcare
- Kids dropping out of school
- Gangs
- Child abuse

If you already have a topic in mind, you can use *listing* to generate supporting details and examples to include in your writing.

▶ VISUALIZING

This is putting yourself in another situation and describing the situation from your point of view. Visualizing can be especially helpful when you are trying to write about another place or time or provide a creative perspective for a topic. For example, you could use visualization to help you explain a technical topic, such as how the human heart works, by visualizing the flow of blood through the different parts of the heart. You could also use visualizing to help you imagine another historical period or for creative writing assignments.

▶ USING CHARTS

Like word maps or webs, charts are ways to group your ideas visually. Some different kinds of charts you might find helpful include

- **Pro and con chart**—to show both sides of an issue or an action plan
- **Five senses chart**—to break an event or situation down into observations

- **Comparison and contrast charts**—to show how things are alike and different
- **Timeline**—to show the chronological relationship between events
- **Flow chart**—to show the steps in a process

Here are some examples of these different kinds of charts.

Example: The pro and con chart below was used by a student to develop ideas in answer to the following writing assignment.

Nuclear energy avoids the mining and pollution problems of traditional fossil fuels. It also poses contamination and health risks. Do you think governments should build nuclear power plants? State your opinion and support it with convincing reasons.

PROS	CONS
Once the plants are built, they can provide low-cost electricity for a long time.	Sometimes they melt down with horrible consequences. (Chernobyl is one example.)
They can allow us to meet our growing energy needs.	Communities near power plants are at greater risk for nuclear contamination.
Nuclear energy avoids the pollution problems of fossil fuels and won't add to global warming problems.	Nuclear wastes build up over time and have to be stored for millions of years.
Safety features and protocols can prevent contamination problems.	Nuclear energy causes other kinds of pollution—thermal pollution to nearby waters, which harms fish.
Nuclear power is virtually unlimited, so it won't run out over time as fossil fuels will.	Not all countries will follow the highest standards of safety.

Example: The five senses chart below was used by a student to develop ideas for a poem about the seashore.

SEE	HEAR	TASTE	FEEL	SMELL
Birds	Ocean	Salt in the air	Cold, wet water	Fresh air
Waves	Gulls		Clammy sand in	Fishy smells
Sand	Waves crashing		between my	Salty air
Waves	Tide		toes	Sea breeze
Shells	Children		Wind blowing my	
Water ebbing	Splashing and		hair in my eyes	
Ocean	laughing in		Scratchy broken	
	the water		shells on the	
			bottoms of my	
			feet	

Example: This comparison and contrast chart was used by a student to develop ideas in answer to the following writing assignment.

Compare a virus with a cell.

VIRUS	CELL
Not living—just an inert particle	Living—smallest unit of life
Must enter a cell in order to replicate—cannot reproduce independently	Can reproduce on its own
Can infect living things and cause diseases	Can infect living things and cause diseases
Tiny—but cannot be seen with a basic compound light microscope	Tiny—but can be seen using a basic compound light microscope
Is made of DNA or RNA	Contains DNA
Uses the same genetic instructions as most life-forms	Uses the same genetic instructions as most other life-forms
Probably left over from cell ancestors	Makes up all living things
Can evolve over time	Can evolve over time

Example: This timeline was used by a student to develop ideas in answer to the following writing assignment.

Trace and describe the main events that occur to a fetus during gestation.

6 weeks	Major organs begin forming
11 weeks	Placenta and umbilical cord are functioning
14 weeks	Baby can smile and frown
16 weeks	Hair, eyebrows, eyelashes are present
18 weeks	Baby can suck thumb
24 weeks	Permanent teeth "buds" begin forming
	End of second trimester
27 weeks	Baby can sense light, smell, taste
31 weeks	Fingernails and toenails are growing
36 weeks	Baby may "drop" into pelvis in preparation for birth
39 weeks	Lungs are mature
	Birth

Example: This flow chart was used by a student to think about the process of resolving an insurance claim after a car accident.

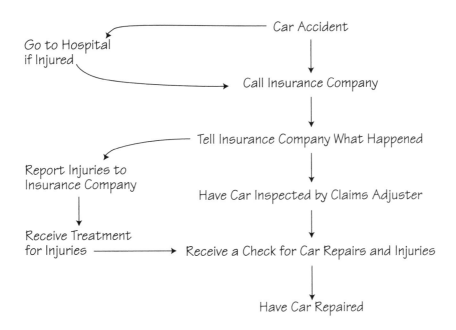

PRACTICE ▶

Check your answers against the answer key at the back of the book.

5. Use any of the strategies discussed in this lesson to generate ideas about the following topic.
Should public school students be required to take sex education classes? Why or why not?

_____

_____

_____

_____

_____

_____

_____

_____

_____

_____

_____

_____

_____

_____

_____

Organizing Your Ideas and Outlining Your Paper

LESSON SUMMARY

This lesson will show you how to organize your ideas logically so that your reader can easily follow. But first, you have to learn how to write a thesis. Then, you will learn different ways of organizing your ideas and sketching out the details you will use to support your thesis. This lesson includes several different ways of organizing your ideas graphically, too.

ow you have a topic and ideas. Are you ready to start writing yet? You may feel like you are ready, but there are two more steps you need to take before you start to make your writing go more smoothly. The first step is developing a tentative thesis statement. The second is organizing your supporting details for your thesis.

▶ WHAT IS A THESIS?

A *thesis statement* is a statement that tells you and your reader what you plan to write about. It is usually one sentence in the introduction to your paper. It tells the main idea of your paper. It might also give the reader an idea of the type of organization and the tone that you plan to use in your paper. Often a thesis statement is an answer to a question. Often it is a statement that you set out to prove. A thesis does not have to be only one sentence long. In some papers, it is appropriate to have a two- or three-sentence thesis.

Before you begin writing, you should have an idea of what your thesis is. You don't have to have the exact thesis statement that you will put in your final paper, but you do need to have the gist written in a tentative form because it lets you organize your thoughts and the rest of the information in your paper.

▶ DEVELOPING A THESIS

When a writing assignment provides the topic, your answer to the question will usually be your thesis. Here are three examples.

Example
Writing assignment: *Describe one of your most important accomplishments in life.*

Tentative thesis: One of my most important accomplishments in life was surviving a winter in Siberia.

Example
You have just studied cancer and cancer cells in your biology class. You teacher gives you the following writing assignment.

Writing assignment: *Think about how cancer cells are different from normal cells. Based on these differences, explain why it has been so difficult to find a cure for cancer.*

Tentative thesis: Cancer cells do not respond to the body's ordinary controls on cell growth and division as normal cells do. Thus, a cure for cancer must prevent cancer cells from dividing uncontrollably while allowing normal cells to divide normally. Finding a way to stop cell growth and division in cancer cells without interfering in normal cell division has proved a difficult task for cancer researchers.

Example
You have just finished reading and discussing the novel *Parrot in the Oven* in your literature class. Your teacher gives you the following writing assignment.

Writing assignment: *Evaluate Mrs. Hernandez as a mother in the novel* Parrot in the Oven. *Do you think Mrs. Hernandez does a good job of raising her children? Would you want her as a mother? Why or why not?*

Tentative thesis: Mrs. Hernandez does a good job of raising her children because she is caring, devoted, and loyal to them. She works hard to keep the family intact, keep their home clean, and put good meals on the table. Moreover, she dreams of a better life for her children and encourages them to take actions that will improve their future.

TEST TAKING TIP

ON A TIMED TEST, you don't have a lot of time to think and plan your writing. A quick way to get started is to simply turn the given question into a thesis statement that answers the question. In the last example, the question begins *Do you think Mrs. Hernandez does a good job of raising her children?*

Some ways to begin a thesis statement for your answer are as follows:

Mrs. Hernandez does a good job of raising her children because . . .

Mrs. Hernandez does not do a good job of raising her children because . . .

Mrs. Hernandez does a terrible job of raising her children because . . .

Often this is a quick and clear way to begin your writing.

What if your writing assignment doesn't give you a question to start with? If your writing assignment is open-ended, you might have to work a little harder at finding a thesis. This is where your topic exploration from the last lesson should come in handy.

A good thesis statement will

- say something that interests both you and your audience.
- be as specific as you can make it.
- focus and narrow your topic.
- address one main idea.
- give your audience a guide to what is coming up.
- help you test your ideas about your topic.
- help you organize what you will say in your paper.
- tell both you and your audience what your conclusion on the topic is.
- often take a position on an issue or answer a question.

Here are some examples of thesis statements.

- Companies should take advantage of the marketing potential of the Internet by advertising and offering customer service via Web pages.
- The U. S. government should support early childhood programs for babies addicted to crack because most of these children are raised in homes lacking adequate stimulation.
- Dr. Stockman's view of mankind and society changes from one of delight to one of disgust as the events of the play "An Enemy of the People" transpire.
- The epilogue of Theseus demonstrates the qualities of a classic Greek mythological hero: physical strength, courage, and morality.
- The scientific stance on the effects of bilingualism on cognitive development have followed the tides of popular belief over the past five decades.
- Throughout *Silas Marner*, George Eliot uses vocabulary, sentence structure, and philosophical commentary to teach her reader a moral.
- Research shows that repeated exposure to air pollution can cause or worsen asthma in children.
- The role of the Indian gods Rudra, Indra, and Varuna in Vedic Indian society show how mankind seeks to escape the worries of the human condition.

THINK ABOUT IT

LET'S TAKE A closer look at a few of these thesis statements. What would you expect to find in a paper that begins with this thesis statement?

The epilogue of Theseus demonstrates the qualities of a classic Greek mythological hero: physical strength, courage, and morality.

Probably you will find a paragraph or a section about each of the qualities listed: physical strength, courage, and morality. The writer will probably try to show how events that are described in the epilogue of Theseus demonstrate these qualities and then relate them to the qualities of a classic Greek mythological hero.

> ### What would you expect to find in a paper that has this thesis statement?
>
> *The scientific stance on the effects of bilingualism on cognitive development have followed the tides of popular belief over the past five decades.*
>
> **The writer will probably show how the conclusions of scientific studies on bilingualism have changed with popular opinion during the last 50 years.**

PRACTICE ▶

Write a tentative thesis for the following writing assignments. Check your answers against the answer key at the back of the book.

1. Your state is considering building a prison close to your home. How do you feel about having a prison near your home?

_____

_____

_____

2. Are uniforms a good idea in the public schools? Why or why not?

_____

_____

_____

3. Describe a time that you got lost. How did you feel? What happened?

_____

_____

_____

4. What would you do if you were President for one day?

_____

_____

_____

► SKETCHING OUT YOUR SUPPORTING DETAILS

Once you have a tentative thesis, it's time to focus on what you want to say about the thesis and how you will support it. The first step is to list the main ideas you want to express in your paper. Then you will need to link each main idea with supporting details. Supporting details are pieces of information that you can use to make your main points. Examples of types of supporting details are listed below.

Types of Supporting Details

Anecdotes—stories or descriptions of experiences you have had or heard about

Examples—specific instances of a general idea

Facts—statements that can be verified in reference materials (such as databases, dictionaries, encyclopedias, college textbooks, or other specialized sources), through interviews with experts, or by making direct observations

Opinions—judgments and predictions, especially those of experts

Quotations—word-for-word statements made by other people, such as experts

Statistics—facts that are written as percentages, ratios, or in other numeric forms

You may already have a list of supporting details in mind. If you aren't sure how each main idea will be supported in your paper, you might go back to your exploratory strategies in Lesson 2. Or, you can list the main ideas on a sheet of paper with supporting details under each main idea.

Another technique would be to organize your main ideas and supporting details graphically. Following are just a few examples of graphic organizers you can use to categorize the information you plan to put in your paper.

Venn diagrams. Venn diagrams are commonly used to show how two or more things are alike and different. This type of diagram might help you organize your supporting details for a comparison and contrast paragraph.

VENN DIAGRAM: to organize similarities and differences

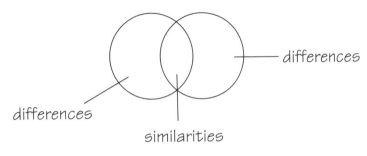

Spider maps. Spider maps are often used to describe one central concept. You might use this type of diagram to organize your supporting details for a paper describing a person or an event. For example, you might use a spider map when writing a paper about a specific character in a piece of literature you have read.

SPIDER MAP: to describe one central concept

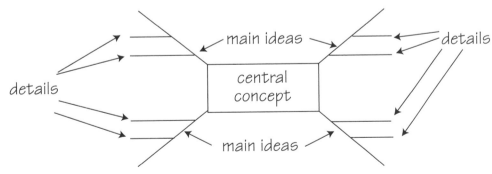

Series maps. Series maps are often used to organize a series of events or the steps in a process. You could use this type of diagram to help you organize the information you plan to put in a how-to paper or to explain a multi-step process.

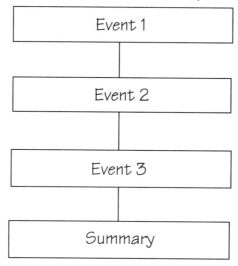

SERIES MAP:
to organize a series of events or steps in a process

| Event 1 |
| Event 2 |
| Event 3 |
| Summary |

Timelines. Timelines are good for organizing chronological information. You might use a timeline to help you organize the information you plan to put in a history paper or to organize the events that lead up to the climax in a novel.

TIMELINE:
to sequence events over time

first event   second event   third event

Hierarchical maps. These diagrams are very typical in composition classes. They are a good way to organize your arguments in a persuasive piece of writing.

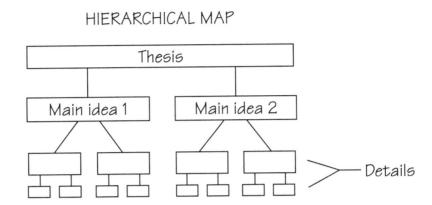

HIERARCHICAL MAP

Sequence charts. Like timelines and series maps, sequence charts can be useful in organizing items that follow a specific sequence, such as events and steps. For example, you could use a sequence chart to organize information about the phases in a scientific process.

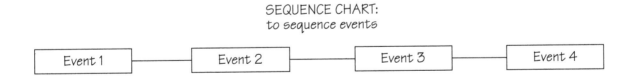

SEQUENCE CHART:
to sequence events

Check your answers against the answer key at the back of the book.

5. Choose one of the thesis statements from the last practice set. Then, use one of the graphic organizers described here to sketch out your supporting details.

IT'S IMPORTANT TO organize your writing in a logical way so that your reader can easily understand what you are saying. Here are some examples of logical organization.

TYPES OF LOGICAL ORGANIZATION

CHRONOLOGICAL OR SEQUENTIAL ORDER—**telling what did, should, or will happen first, second, third, and so on**

CAUSE AND EFFECT—**telling how events (causes) result in other events (effects) or telling about events (effects) and then explaining why they happened (causes)**

COMPARE AND CONTRAST—**telling how ideas are alike and different**

ORDER OF DEGREE—**telling how different ideas can be ranked in importance, familiarity, complexity, and so on**

SPATIAL ORDER—**telling how things are arranged in space (for example, top to bottom, bottom to top, near to far, inside out, and so on)**

You can use these organizational structures for your entire paper, or just for a portion of your paper. You might choose more than one structure, depending on the purpose of different parts of your paper.

► A WORD ABOUT OUTLINES

You've probably been asked to write an outline for a paper before, and this thought might make you cringe. If you've gotten this far in the prewriting process, however, you probably already have an outline—an informal one. If you have a tentative thesis and have sketched out your main ideas and supporting details in a graphic organizer, in a list, or in any way that makes sense to you, then you have an informal outline. An outline is just a guide for what you will say in your paper.

A more formal outline might look like this one.

> THESIS: Anthony's funeral oration in the play *Julius Caesar* shows several forms of emotional appeal.
>
> I. He captures his audience's attention by repeating nice ideas that are contrary to his intentions.
> II. He plays on the crowd's impatience and creates a sense of curiosity and anxiety.
> III. He makes the audience feel ashamed for the bad way they've treated the dead Caesar.
> IV. He uses emotionally charged words and examples of Caesar's good qualities to show that Caesar was not that ambitious.
>
> CONCLUSION: Anthony uses several forms of emotionalism to manipulate his audience.

Why should you bother making an outline before writing? First, an outline helps you think through what you will say, so it can save you time when you actually start writing. In addition, it can show omissions in your paper. An outline can even help you avoid writer's block! One of the most important reasons to do an outline before you start writing is to help you evaluate your thesis. Is your thesis narrow enough? Is it too broad? Can you support it adequately? Here's how to use your outline to test your prewriting material.

- If you have more to say than you can fit in your outline, you probably need to refocus your thesis statement. It's too broad.
- If you can't find enough to say in your outline, your thesis is probably too narrow. You should consider making it broader.
- If you've tried different ways of exploring and researching your topic and you still can't find enough evidence to support your thesis, you should reconsider your thesis. You might want to write a new thesis that you can support.
- If your outline is still sound after putting it to this test, then you are ready to start writing.

Check your answers against the answer key at the back of the book.

6. Go back to the work you did in question 5. Write up your thesis and supporting statements in outline style.

_____

_____

_____

_____

_____

_____

_____

_____

_____

_____

_____

_____

_____

_____

_____

_____

7. Now use the outline you wrote in question 6 to evaluate your thesis. Is your thesis broad enough? Narrow enough? Can you support it adequately? Explain your answer.

_____

_____

_____

_____

_____

_____

_____

_____

_____

_____

_____

_____

_____

_____

_____

_____

_____

_____

_____

_____

Start Writing!
The Drafting Process

▶ Drafting Your Paper

LESSON SUMMARY

By now, you've done a lot of work on your assignment and you're probably feeling pretty ready to start writing. This lesson will show you how to get started writing. It will explain the drafting process and give you tips on how to begin a first draft of your paper. You will learn how to write topic sentences and paragraphs. You will also learn how to overcome writer's block.

o, you have a topic and an outline and you're ready to start writing. You know what you want to say. And you have an idea of how you would like to say it. What's next? Drafting.

▶ WHAT IS DRAFTING?

Drafting means writing a rough, or scratch, form of your paper. It's a time to really focus on the main ideas you want to get across in your paper. When drafting, you might skip sections or make notes to yourself to come back and add more examples in certain spots or to check your facts later. As you draft, you don't need to worry about grammar, spelling, or punctuation. You will have time to refine these mechanical parts of your paper at a later stage.

You are probably familiar with the term *rough draft*. A rough draft is the first version of your paper. It won't be perfect and it won't be final. It's not the version you will show your audience. It's not usually the version you are graded on in class. It's a start, though. And it will form the foundation for your final paper, so it's important that you do a good job even though you know it's just a start.

YOU MAY BE THINKING, "I have to write more than one draft of my paper?" Your first draft is usually considered a rough draft. It certainly won't be your best draft. So, how many drafts should you plan to write? It will depend on the writing assignment, your time frame, and essentially on you.

In a timed situation, you may have time to write only one or two drafts. When given weeks or a semester to complete a writing assignment, you should plan to have several drafts. That means, of course, that you will have to begin early—waiting until the last minute can cut into the number of drafts you can write.

Don't think for a minute that drafting is more work than just writing your paper once. First, writing a good paper takes time. As you become a better drafter and writer, you will find that you are more efficient and productive than you used to be. The results of your work will be better, and you will spend less time staring at blank pages, wondering what to do. Finally, be sensible: although each draft will usually be an improvement over the last draft, there is a point of diminishing returns.

▶ DRAFTING STRATEGIES

Open any book or newspaper, and you'll see right away that the text is divided into paragraphs. Essentially, your job in the drafting process is to translate your outline—along with other good ideas you have along the way—into paragraphs. So let's review paragraphs quickly.

- **Paragraphs usually begin with a topic sentence.** The topic sentence tells the reader the main idea of the paragraph. It doesn't have to come first. And it might not even be stated explicitly in the paragraph. But all the sentences in the paragraph should relate to one main idea. Do your reader a favor and make it clear what your main idea is—this will avoid misunderstandings.

- **Coherent paragraphs flow from sentence to sentence.** This means that the sentences are linked to each other logically. You might organize the sentences in a paragraph according to chronological or sequential order, by cause and effect, by comparison and contrast, in order of degree, or in spatial order.

- **Good paragraphs include details that support the main idea.** Supporting details include anecdotes, examples, facts, opinions, quotations, and/or statistics that back up the paragraph's main idea.

Let's compare the paragraph below, in which a writer describes himself at work, with the elements of a good paragraph listed above.

The paragraph begins with a topic sentence.

I am the kind of person who gets things done—correctly, professionally, on time, on budget. My supervisors trust important projects and tasks in my hands, and coworkers often seek my advice on handling situations at work. Clients with whom I work outside my office say that my expectations and the materials I send them are very clear, organized, and thorough. I have the reputation at work as someone who works tirelessly to solve problems, always follows through, and rarely takes no for an answer without a valid explanation. I am analytical, focused, organized, dependable, responsible, and determined to do a good job. Overall, I am a very competent person.

The paragraph flows from sentence to sentence. He systematically describes the impressions of each group of people he interacts with at work—supervisors, coworkers, clients.

The paragraph includes details that support the main idea.

There are many ways to begin drafting a paper into paragraphs. One way is to translate the main points of your outline into topic sentences, and then to develop each topic sentence into a paragraph. Or, you can draft paragraph by paragraph, beginning with a topic sentence and then supporting it. You might use a graphic organizer like this one to begin drafting.

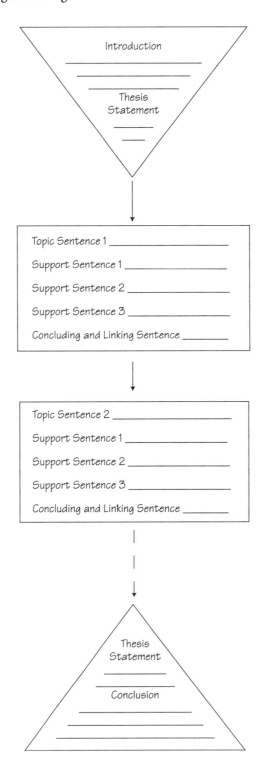

WRITING TIP

AS YOU BEGIN writing, feel free to try different approaches and angles. This is a good time to experiment with your writing tone, style, and form. At the same time, you should focus on

▶ supporting your thesis statement
▶ presenting your information in an easy-to-follow way
▶ staying on your topic

If you are finding it hard to do any of these three things, then you might want to reconsider your thesis statement, outline, or even your topic. Would adjustments to these items make your drafting flow more smoothly?

PRACTICE ▶

1. Choose one of the thesis statements from Lesson 3, and write two or three topic sentences that you could use for paragraphs in a rough draft.

_____
_____
_____
_____
_____
_____

2. Choose one of the thesis statements from Lesson 3, and write a paragraph that could go anywhere in a rough draft.

_____
_____
_____
_____
_____
_____
_____
_____
_____
_____
_____
_____
_____

▶ OVERCOMING WRITER'S BLOCK

Everyone has a hard time getting started once in a while. Don't waste time staring at a blank page and fretting. Instead, try these techniques to get your draft started.

- **Start where you feel inspired**—you don't have to start at the beginning. You can start in the middle or go on to a new section of your paper if you've gotten stuck in one spot.
- **Try one of the prewriting strategies from Lesson 3.** For example, you can freewrite on one section of your outline or one paragraph of your paper.
- **Summarize your main point.** Write what you most want to say in as simple language as you can. This might be as easy as revising your thesis statement or working on your favorite point in the paper.
- **Change your perspective.** Begin your draft as a letter to someone else or write as if you were someone else.
- **Try something different.** If you are used to composing on the computer, pick up a pen and paper instead.
- **Talk it out.** Explain to someone else what you want to say. Bouncing your ideas off them can help you clarify your thoughts. Besides, they might say things that will spur your writing.
- **Visualize yourself writing successfully.** Imagine that you are in a comfortable spot surrounded by all the things you need to write—and are busy writing.
- **Stop what you are doing.** Go on to another assignment or another activity. Wait an hour or so, or if you have time, a day or so, before returning to your writing. You'll come back with a fresh outlook and usually overcome the problem easily.

HERE ARE SOME good habits to start as you draft.

- **Refer to your thesis statement and your assignment regularly.** You might want to even keep them in view as you write.
- **Use your outline as a guide.** As you write, go back to your outline. It will help you stay focused and organized. However, if while drafting you come up with a better idea or better way to organize your ideas, don't feel pinned down by your outline. Be flexible.
- **Keep a copy of each draft you write.** Don't throw away something that you need later.

▶ **Make a slush file.** If you come up with ideas or write paragraphs that aren't fitting into your paper, but you like them, you don't have to throw them away. Tuck them away in a folder for later use. Your folder can be a paper one or one on a computer disk that you can search electronically. You may never come back to your slush file, or you may need it later in the drafting or revising stages of your paper. A slush file is also a good place to start when you are looking for topic ideas for new writing assignments or trying to overcome writer's block.

LESSON

6

▶ # Convincing Your Reader

LESSON SUMMARY

If you're tempted to skip this lesson because you aren't working on a persuasive writing assignment, hold on for a just a second. Have you ever read a science fiction novel? If you really got into the story, the author did a good job of convincing you of the setting, so the story could seem credible under the assumptions she or he set up. In fact, it's important to be convincing no matter what kind of writing you are undertaking. This lesson will show you how to make your writing more convincing. You will learn how to establish your credibility as a writer. You'll also learn techniques you can use to persuade your reader of your viewpoint.

Papers that take a stand or whose purpose is to persuade the reader of a specific point of view need more than supporting details and good writing; they also have to be convincing. Even if you aren't writing a persuasive piece, there are things you can do to establish your credibility with your reader and build your reader's confidence in the ideas you express.

▶ WHAT IS CREDIBILITY?

Let's say you are reading a book about a topic you know a lot about. You are reading along and suddenly the writer says something that you know is absolutely incorrect! What do you do? You might stop reading right there and throw the book away. You might begin questioning ideas in the book that you would have believed before. What has happened? You no longer trust this writer. The writer has lost his or her credibility with you. If you want others to believe what you write and to try to follow your ideas, you must establish credibility. This is true of any kind of writing you are undertaking.

▶ ESTABLISHING YOUR CREDIBILITY

Here are some things you can do to establish credibility.

- **Put yourself in your reader's shoes.** Think about the background, assumptions, and point of view of your reader. Try to anticipate objections and questions that will pop into your reader's mind as he or she reads your paper. If you're writing a story, make sure the ending follows earlier events in the story and the characters are true to your descriptions of them. If you're writing a letter to the editor of a newspaper, address the opinions of the readership. If you're writing a letter of inquiry about interviewing for a job, show how your background matches the qualifications of the position you are interested in.

- **Be honest.** Don't put forth claims you can't back up. Don't make up stuff that's not true. Don't exaggerate. When you do these things, you lose your credibility whether you're writing a persuasive essay or a cover letter for a job.

- **Give those who have a different opinion credit where it's due.** Don't ignore good points just because they poke holes in your argument. Acknowledge and defuse counter-arguments when possible.

- **Use expert opinions to support your ideas.** Experience and prestigious reputations usually mean greater credibility. So when you quote experts or use statistics, tell your reader briefly where you got the information. Use titles and full names of experts and their affiliations. When possible, include a brief description of who the person is or what the organization is. The telling, in itself, lets your reader know that you have paid attention to the credentials of your sources and lends credibility to you. And don't forget to tell your reader about your own expertise on a topic.

- **Use credible sources.** All expert opinions are not equally credible. Don't use an astrologist's opinion to back up a medical argument. Don't use a quotation from the Bible to support a scientific claim. Although people who have similar beliefs will accept these sources, you will lose credibility with the rest of your audience.

Here are some things you should try to avoid doing because they weaken your credibility.

- **Try to avoid bias.** Of course, you are biased when you take a stand on an issue. But you need to try to be even-handed. No matter the purpose of your writing, you need to be careful about appearing biased. When you use biased language or ideas, your reader will begin to question how clearly you are able to think about the topic.

- **Try to avoid offending your audience.** Be sensitive in your choice of words and in the ways you characterize others. Show respect for other cultures and opinions even if you do not agree with them.

- **Try to avoid making absolute statements.** Absolute statements include the words *all, always, never, none,* and so on. Use these words very carefully. Just because you can't think of an exception to an absolute statement doesn't mean one doesn't exist or that your reader won't think of one immediately.

HERE ARE SOME ways to avoid absolute statements in your writing.

INSTEAD OF WRITING THIS	TRY ONE OF THESE
All	**Many** **Most** **Nearly all** **The majority of** **Some**
None	**Few or very few** **A fraction of** **Almost none** **With few exceptions** **Hardly any**
Always	**Sometimes** **Often** **Usually** **Frequently** **Almost always**
Never	**Rarely** **Infrequently** **Hardly ever**

▶ MAKING A GOOD ARGUMENT

Many types of writing actually require you to persuade your audience. You may be writing a letter to the editor of a publication, a cover letter for a job, an essay for application to college, a grant proposal, or a persuasive writing assignment. In all of these situations, you will need to make a convincing argument.

Here are the basic steps to making a good argument:

- **Introduce and explain the issue.** Your reader may or may not be familiar with the issue. If they are not, you need to provide a balanced overview of it. Even if they are familiar with the issue, they will judge your credibility by how you define the issue.
- **Take a stand.** Tell your reader where you stand on the issue. Usually this is done in your thesis statement.
- **Give supporting reasons for your position.** Tell your reader why they should agree with you or why they should support your cause. Use specific evidence: facts, quotations, statistics, and so on.

- **Refute opposing arguments.** Tell your reader why the other side is misguided, or why your position makes more sense.
- **Concede the valid points of other positions.** Don't try to ignore or hide the facts when they aren't on your side.
- **Conclude logically.** Show how your conclusion stems logically from your position and the evidence you've provided.

Now let's look at a persuasive essay and see these steps in action.

Intro-duce the issue.

We hear in the news all the time that American public schools are failing our students—American students are not competing favorably on international tests and schools seem to be faring worse all the time. Are our schools really doing worse today than in the past? Actually, American schools are doing a better job today than in the past.

Take a stand. This is also the writer's thesis.

Concede valid points.

First, why don't American students do better on international tests? It's a fact that European and Asian countries, even war-torn and third-world countries, often do better than American high school students on math and science tests. How is this possible? When looking at the scores, we must examine who is taking the tests. In the early grades, a broad cross section of students in all countries are pretty much taking the tests. If you look at the scores, you'll see that the United States gets the top marks at this point. Starting in high school, however, the United States's scores plummet. It's also around high school that European and Asian schools have weeded out less-capable students from their education systems. However, American high schools include all students: those who are academically talented, those who don't speak English, those who are handicapped, and so on. So the comparison is not fair. The international tests compare the most talented European and Asian students with a broad cross section of American students.

Refute opposing arguments. The writer explains why the international test scores are not a good indicator of public school performance in the United States.

Give supporting reasons. The writer gives evidence to support her position that American public schools are doing a better job today than in the past.

Even if we discount international comparisons, however, it sometimes seems as though schools are still doing a worse job today than they were in 1950. Is this true? No, it's not. Let's look first at domestic standardized test scores. In 1995, 75% more students scored above 650 on the SAT Math test than in 1941. If you factor out the Asian-American population, 57% of African-American, Hispanic, and white students did better on the SAT Math in 1995 than in 1941. The norms for the SAT Math test were the same between 1941 and 1995, so the higher scores are comparable. Test scores on the ACT college entrance exam have also increased each of the last three years.

Do test scores really mean that schools are doing a better job? Let's look at other indicators of success. First, students are learning more at school now than in the past. If you visit your local high school, you'll find that many students are taking college credit courses in high school. In fact, a high school student can begin college as a junior just based on coursework completed in high school. Today, students are expected to learn at least fifty more years of history than in 1950—and in the same amount of time. Major events have occurred during the last 50 years—including the Korean War, the Vietnam War, the fall of communism. Calculus used to be college math—now most high schools offer two years of Calculus. DNA had not been discovered in 1950. Today, DNA, genetic engineering, and a host of other topics are standard fare in a first-year biology course—that's a course that typically includes a textbook with more than 50 chapters and 1000 pages. In 1950, we classified all living things as either plants or animals; today, living things are classified into six different kingdoms, and some scientists are already postulating as many as eleven different kinds of life. On top of standard academics, students are also learning computer literacy and computer programming. Students are learning more academically today than ever before.

Give supporting reasons. The writer gives evidence to support her position that American public schools are doing a better job today than in the past.

In addition, graduation rates are rising. In 1870, only about 3% of high school students graduated from high school. In 1995, 83% did, and 60% of those went on to college. So more students are graduating and going to college, too.

If public schools are doing so well, why are Americans unhappy with them? Americans feel that schools are doing a bad job because they aren't meeting the needs of their kids. But which needs are we talking about? That all depends on the child—and every child is different. The problem is there is no consensus on the criteria upon which our schools are to be judged. If a child is athletically inclined, a school should provide a strong athletic program and opportunities for that child to gain an athletic scholarship to college. Handicapped students need special programs, too. In fact, every child requires something special, and so the schools are left meeting too many needs.

Concede valid points. The writer validates the feelings of many parents who are unhappy with public schools.

This is not a new issue. Even in the 1950s and 1960s, newspapers were filled with articles complaining about the poor quality of American schools. In fact, our discontent stems from a conflict inherent in the American mentality. We are torn between our democratic principles of providing a free and appropriate education for everyone and achieving excellence. As Americans, we do

Explain the issue. The writer explains why people are unhappy with schools even though the schools are doing a better job today than in the past.

not want to leave any child out, and so federal law mandates that all public schools must accept all students and meet their needs, including non-academic needs. Public schools provide breakfast and lunch for students, accommodations and self-sufficiency training for handicapped students; public schools even bathe students and administer feeding tubes to those who can't eat. At the same time, we want the best for our children. Public schools are expected to provide special education, athletic, gifted and talented, vocational, music, and art programs, too, whereas our international competitors focus only on academics. We are not happy with our schools—even though they do so much more than those in other countries—because they are not perfect.

Schools are working harder and meeting more needs today than ever before. Our schools are doing a better job than they did in the past—even though it may sometimes seem otherwise. Will Rogers summed it up well: "The schools are not as good as they used to be—and they never were."

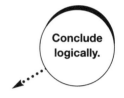
Conclude logically.

▶ EXPLAINING YOUR REASONING

Explaining and supporting the reasons you give for your position are perhaps the best ways to convince your audience. Here are three strategies for strengthening this part of your writing.

- Show the progression of your argument as you write.
- Give strong examples and details that support your position.
- Explain how your examples and supporting details relate to your argument.

Let's look again at how the writer gives her supporting reasons in one paragraph from the last essay.

Show the progression of your argument. Here, the writer explains that there are many indicators of success and that she is not relying only on test scores.

Do test scores really mean that schools are doing a better job? Let's look at other indicators of success. First, students are learning more at school now than in the past. If you visit your local high school, you'll find that many students are taking college credit courses in high school. In fact, a high school student can begin college as a junior just based on coursework completed in high school. Today, students are expected to learn at least fifty more years of history than in 1950—and in the same amount of time. Major events have occurred during the last 50 years—including the Korean War, the Vietnam War, the fall of communism. Calculus used to be college math—now most high schools offer two years of Calculus. DNA had not been discovered in 1950. Today, DNA, genetic engineering, and a host of other

Use strong evidence. The writer compares what students learn in school today with what they've learned in the past. She structures her essay school subject by school subject.

Show how your examples and supporting details relate to your argument. The writer sums up the evidence she's listed.

topics are standard fare in a first-year biology course—that's a course that typically includes a textbook with more than 50 chapters and 1,000 pages. In 1950, we classified all living things as either plants or animals; today, living things are classified into six different kingdoms, and some scientists are already postulating as many as eleven different kinds of life. On top of standard academics, students are also learning computer literacy and computer programming. Students are learning more academically today than ever before.

PRACTICE ▶

1. Choose one of the topics below. Then write a thesis statement and supporting reasons that you could use to convince your reader of your position on the issue.
    - Should people with certain medical conditions be allowed legal access to marijuana?
    - Choose a book you read recently. Would you recommend this book to a friend? Why or why not?
    - Explain why voters should support a certain candidate in an upcoming election.

2. Use the information you listed in question 1 above to write a persuasive paragraph.

Beginning and Ending Your Paper

LESSON SUMMARY

Imagine you are meeting someone for the first time. They shake your hand firmly, smile, make eye contact, and greet you in a way that makes you instantly feel comfortable. This person has just made a good first impression on you. And that's exactly what you want to do in the introduction to your paper—you want to make a good first impression on your reader. This lesson will give you strategies for beginning your paper in a way that makes a good impression on your reader. It will also show you how to conclude your paper effectively.

The introduction and conclusion are perhaps the most important parts of your paper. You want to make a good first impression in the introduction. The purpose of the conclusion is to leave your reader with a favorable impression and your message.

▶ WRITING THE INTRODUCTION

The introduction to your paper should set the stage for the rest of the paper. It's here that a reader will decide whether or not to keep reading. So, this is your chance to convince your reader to keep reading. It's also your chance to clearly tell your reader what your paper is about. Your introduction should accomplish two main goals.

- Get your reader's attention.
- Present and explain your thesis statement.

TO GET YOUR reader's attention, consider beginning your paper with one of these.

- **Interesting or surprising facts**
- **A vivid description**
- **A question**
- **An anecdote**
- **A quotation**
- **A stance on an issue**

Let's look at two examples of introductions.

Example 1

Gets the reader's attention. The writer begins with an introduction that hints at danger and clearly draws the reader in.

In spite of his father's and his mother's repeated warning about the lake and the rushing water beneath it, Matt went ice skating with his cousins on a frigid winter morning last March. He often did things he was told not to do. Like the time he took off on his motorbike in the rain. Or the time he insisted on walking home well past dark. But this time was life threatening, and even his friends doubted his common sense.

Present and explain your thesis statement. The writer repeats the idea of danger in the last sentence.

Example 2

Present and explain your thesis statement. The writer clearly states she is going to show that Pepys wrote for personal reasons, not to attain fame.

No one knows for sure why Samuel Pepys wrote his diary. Upon his death, he arranged for the six leather-bound volumes to be deposited at Cambridge, along with a key to his shorthand manuscript. Because of this and other events, some scholars say that Pepys wrote his diaries with the intention of becoming famous after his death. However, my analysis of Samuel Pepys and his diaries suggests that he wrote for purely personal reasons.

Get the reader's attention. The writer begins with background information about the controversy over why Samuel Pepys wrote his diaries.

1. Read the introductions to three different pieces of writing. They can come from a newspaper, your own writing, a magazine, a classmate's writing, and so on. Then, answer the questions below.

 a. How did each piece get your attention?

_____

_____

_____

 b. What is the thesis statement of each piece?

_____

_____

_____

_____

_____

2. Read the following introduction to a persuasive essay. Then answer the questions below.

> Despite the heated debate among evolutionists and Creationists, the two ideas are very similar. Dr. Dobzhansky, author of *Mankind Evolving*, even goes so far as to say, "Christianity is a religion that is implicitly evolutionistic, in that it believes history to be meaningful." In fact, evolution and Creation can be combined and accepted as one general explanation of mankind's origin. These two explanations are not in conflict with one another, but actually need one another in order to complete the answer to mankind's questions.

 a. Does the introduction get your attention? Explain your answer.

_____

_____

_____

_____

 b. What is the thesis statement?

_____

_____

 c. Would you continue to read the rest of this essay? Why or why not?

_____

_____

_____

_____

3. Choose one of the thesis statements you fleshed out in an earlier lesson. Then, use the strategies in this lesson to write an introduction to the paper. Use the blank pages at the end of this book for your work.

▶ WRITING THE CONCLUSION

Your conclusion is your last opportunity to tell your reader your message. It's usually the last thing he or she will read. Your conclusion should accomplish these goals:

- Remind your reader of your thesis statement.
- Summarize the main ideas of your paper.
- Give your reader a take-home message.

What is a take-home message? It's the most important message you'd like for people to come away from your paper with. One way to come up with your take-home message is to ask yourself this question: *If I could choose only one thing for my reader to remember, take home, and share with others, what would it be?* This is the message you want to include in your conclusion.

WRITING TIP

Here are some ways to conclude your paper:

▶ **Spur the reader to action**

▶ **Suggest a course of action**

▶ **Generalize to a broader situation**

▶ **Make a prediction about the future**

▶ **Ask your reader a question**

▶ **Use a thoughtful quotation or anecdote**

Let's look at an example of a conclusion.

Summarize the main ideas of your paper. The writer refers to problems she has discussed earlier in the paper and reminds the reader that she was able to turn those situations around.

Remind your reader of your thesis statement. The writer restates her thesis statement.

I was able to overcome a number of obstacles during my year abroad. My trip could have easily been a disaster when confronted with any one of these problems. It was not because I was able to make the experience enriching to myself as well as to many of the people I encountered. It was this experience that encouraged me to study Chinese and Russian and to live in Taiwan and in Russia. It was also this experience that convinced me that I could do anything that I put my mind to.

Give your reader a take-home message. The writer makes a generalization about herself based on what she learned from her experience abroad.

4. Read the conclusions to three different pieces of writing. They can come from a newspaper, your own writing, a magazine, a classmate's writing, and so on. Then, answer the questions below.

a. Do they restate the thesis statement?

_____

_____

b. Do they summarize the main points of the piece?

_____

_____

c. What is the take-home message of each piece?

_____

_____

_____

_____

_____

_____

5. Choose one of the thesis statements you fleshed out in an earlier lesson. Then use the strategies in this lesson to write a conclusion to the paper.

Evaluating What You've Written— Revising and Editing

Revising Your Paper

LESSON SUMMARY

So you've written at least one draft of your paper. You're feeling pretty happy with the result. What's next? This lesson will show you how to evaluate what you've written and make improvements. It will explain the revising process and give you tips on making your paper the best it can be.

ou might feel as though you should be done with your paper by now. You *are* close to the end! But you would be wise to take some time to evaluate what you've written to make sure your paper says what you meant to say.

▶ REVIEWING WHAT YOU'VE WRITTEN

As you read the first draft of your paper, you might come across a number of problems. For example, you might find misspelled words or confusing sentences. You might find that your thesis isn't supported adequately. One way to review your paper is to tackle different levels of problems at different times. Here are three main levels to look at.

- **Content:** What the paper says
- **Structure:** How the paper reads (this will be addressed in the next lesson)
- **Mechanics:** How the paper is written—spelling, grammar, punctuation, and usage (this will be addressed in Lesson 10)

It's convenient to begin with the big picture—the content—then to work your way down to other types of problems. In this lesson, you will learn how to evaluate your paper's content. Ask yourself these questions as you first begin to review your paper.

- Does my paper do what the assignment asks?
- Is my thesis statement clear and easy to understand?
- Have I supported my thesis statement in a convincing way?

LET'S QUICKLY ADDRESS each of these questions.

Does my paper do what the assignment asks? Reread your assignment. Focus on what the assignment asks you to do and how it asks you to do it. Is your topic appropriate to the assignment? If a topic is given, do you address all its parts? If your paper does not meet the requirements of the assignment, then you will have to rewrite at least some parts of your paper. Before revising, though, be sure you understand the assignment so you will not go astray again.

Is my thesis statement clear and easy to understand? Find your thesis statement. Is it clear? Does it tell what you intend for the rest of the paper to say? If you can't find a clear thesis statement, your thesis statement doesn't tell what you intend for the rest of the paper to say, or you have more than one thesis statement, then you have some work to do.

Have I supported my thesis statement in a convincing way? Do you have specific examples, facts, reasons, or other details that support your thesis statement? Are your supporting statements directly related to your thesis statement? Do you have some statements that are not supported? If your thesis statement is not adequately supported, then you have some revising to do.

► THE REVISING PROCESS

Everyone has his or her own method for revising a paper. As you become a more experienced writer, you will develop ways that work for you. Here are the basic steps involved in revising the content of your paper.

1. **Read your paper very carefully and very critically as if you were the intended audience.** Sometimes, it's helpful to read your paper aloud. This is the time to judge what the paper says. As you read, ask yourself the questions from the Content Revision Checklist.

Content Revision Checklist
- Does the introduction clearly explain what the paper is about? Does it prepare the reader for what comes next?
- Is the thesis statement clear?
- Does each paragraph relate to the thesis statement?
- Are the main ideas—topic sentences—related to the thesis statement? Do they back it up?
- Do the paragraphs support the thesis statement? Is the support specific? Is it convincing?
- Does the conclusion logically end the paper? Does it give a take-home message that stems from the rest of the paper?
- Overall, does the paper meet the goals of the assignment? Does it meet personal goals?

WRITING TIP

IT'S USUALLY EASIER to read your work critically if you allow some time to pass in between the drafting and the revising phases. It's very difficult to see the flaws in a paper that you have just written. Make sure you begin writing early enough to allow some time to pass before you begin revising the paper.

2. **Decide what needs to be done.** You may decide to write an entirely new draft, if, for example, your paper does not fulfill your assignment. Or, you may decide that the draft you have can be easily fixed with some minor revisions.

3. **Make the needed changes.** It may be helpful to review the drafting process from the last section again before making the changes. What kinds of changes are made at this stage?
   - You may need to add supporting statements.
   - You may need to delete parts that don't really support your thesis statement or sentences that repeat things you've already said once.

- You may need to replace parts that are not clear or that you have cut.
- You may need to move sentences or paragraphs around so they make more sense.

PRACTICE ▶

1. Following the Content Revision Checklist on page 75, read, then evaluate the following essay.

As I exited the plane with my classmates, I realized that relying on each other's strengths would be essential to our visit in Russia. Throughout the ten months that I spent in Russia, studying, traveling, working, and adapting to a new world, I learned some valuable lessons—assumptions differ across cultures, my way is not the only way, and be prepared for the unknown.

As an exchange student in St. Petersburg, I had to overcome daily cultural, linguistic, and physical challenges. Each of these challenges taught me the important lesson of being flexible in planning when dealing with others. I was able to witness many changes in the country during my stay.

When I came home from Russia, I was elected President of the Russian Club. As President, I took on a project to record a Russian textbook to cassette tapes for students who are visually impaired. I recruited 15 volunteers and trained them on the recorders. Then, I developed a schedule for the volunteers and set down reading guidelines. We completed the project ahead of schedule.

I am currently a Team Leader at work. I manage a team of customer service representatives. Being a team leader has honed my communication, management, organizational, leadership, and team skills. Deciding how to reorganize teams with other managers and successfully complete team restructuring with changing staff has become commonplace. Completing daily reports has allowed me to track trends and adjust office procedures or teams as needed. By training and mentoring coworkers, I have gained the reputation of being a trusted resource and leader in my office.

The skills that I have learned from the many trips I have taken will allow me to succeed in the business technology program at Johnson Community College. This certificate will give me the skills to further my career, and I will be an asset to companies in managing changes in technology.

a. Does the introduction clearly explain what the paper is about? Does it prepare the reader for what comes next?

_____

_____

_____

b. Is the thesis statement clear? What is the thesis statement?

_____

_____

_____

c. Does each paragraph relate to the thesis statement?

_____

_____

_____

d. Are the main ideas—topic sentences—related to the thesis statement? Do they back it up?

_____

_____

_____

e. Do the paragraphs support the thesis statement? Is the support specific? Is it convincing?

_____

_____

_____

f. Does the conclusion logically end the paper? Does it give a take-home message that stems from the rest of the paper?

_____

_____

_____

g. How might this paper be improved?

_____

_____

_____

_____

_____

2. Choose a draft of one of your own papers. Then, use the Content Revision Checklist on page 75 to evaluate your paper and revise one of the paragraphs.

GETTING OTHERS TO READ YOUR PAPER

You should definitely read and review your own work. After all, you are the only one who really knows what you want your paper to say. However, sometimes it's also helpful to have others read your paper. They can tell you if you are getting your points across, as well as give you their general impression of the paper. Here are some people you might want to ask to read your paper:

- your peers or classmates
- your friends
- your family
- your teachers
- the staff at your school's writing center

Remember, you are asking for others' impressions of your paper. It's not academically honest to have others rewrite or revise your paper for you, but you might ask them these types of questions about your paper:

- What parts do you like best?
- What do you think is the main message of the paper?
- Are any parts of the paper confusing to you? Unclear? Too long? Hard to follow?
- What could I do to make this a better paper?

Keep in mind that you are asking these people for their time. Make sure that you give them the best version of your paper that you can write. Don't give them a very rough or sloppy paper to sort through. Make their job as easy and painless as possible.

Finally, just because someone tells you to make a change in your paper, doesn't mean you need to make that change. Before you modify your paper based on someone else's feedback, make sure that the revisions meet your goals for the paper.

Checking the Focus and Organization of Your Paper

LESSON SUMMARY

Have you ever listened to a debate on the radio or on television and thought, "That person has some good points, but I'm not sure how they relate to the question?" Although you might have enjoyed listening to the person talk, you were probably also frustrated because you didn't know what he or she would say next or why. To avoid frustrating your reader and to make sure your reader can follow your message, you'll want to make sure your paper is well-organized and focused. In this lesson, you'll learn some strategies for checking and improving the organization and focus of your paper.

In the last lesson, you learned how to look at your paper as a whole and revise the content. In this lesson, you will learn how to look at the paragraphs in your paper. You'll learn to look for two main things: focus and organization.

▶ CHECKING THE FOCUS

Remember from Lesson 5 that a good paragraph has a topic sentence. The topic sentence tells the reader the main idea of the paragraph. All the other sentences in the paragraph should relate to that main idea. A paragraph that does this is said to be *focused*. It has one main idea. How can you tell if your paragraphs are focused? First, you should read each paragraph by itself. Then, look for these things in each paragraph.

- Does the paragraph have a topic sentence? (Not all paragraphs have a topic sentence. Sometimes the topic sentence is implied.)
- What is the main idea of the paragraph? (Even if the topic sentence is not explicitly written, you should be able to determine the main idea based on the information given in the paragraph.)
- Do all the sentences in the paragraph support the main idea?

Let's use these questions to evaluate a paragraph from a paper.

Example

> **Does the paragraph have a topic sentence? Yes, here it is.**

Have you ever thought about getting a tattoo? If so, then you need to know that tattoos can cause health problems. Tattoo parlors can spread germs through equipment that is not properly sterilized. That means you could get hepatitis—a serious liver disease—or even AIDS just by getting a tattoo. People who have AIDS face many more health problems as well as discrimination. The dyes used to make a tattoo on your skin can also spread germs. Even if a tattoo parlor uses sterile equipment and dyes, the tattoo still breaks a person's skin, which means your body is open to germs until the skin heals. Before you get a tattoo, think about the health risks.

> **What is the main idea of the paragraph? The paragraph is about the health hazards of getting a tattoo.**

> **Do all the sentences in the paragraph support the main idea? This sentence should probably be deleted because it isn't relevant to the paragraph's main idea.**

PRACTICE ▶

1. Evaluate the following paragraph by answering these questions.

> There are two main things that I really dislike about myself. First, I am a bashful person. For example, I am really shy when called on in class or required to speak in front of an audience. Often, I will even become embarrassed and blush while talking on the phone to a stranger. I'm also constantly searching for acceptance from my peers. I try very hard to please my friends, family, boss, and teachers. Sometimes, I will even do things that I don't particularly enjoy because I think it pleases others.

a. Does the paragraph have a topic sentence? If so, what is it?

_____

_____

_____

b. What is the main idea of the paragraph?

_____

_____

_____

c. Do all the sentences in the paragraph support the main idea?

_____

_____

_____

2. Now choose a paragraph from one of your own drafts. Evaluate the paragraph by answering these questions.

   a. Does the paragraph have a topic sentence? If so, what is it?

   _____

   _____

   _____

   b. What is the main idea of the paragraph?

   _____

   _____

   _____

   c. Do all the sentences in the paragraph support the main idea?

   _____

   _____

   _____

▶ CHECKING THE ORGANIZATION

You may have heard people talk about a paragraph "flowing." Largely, they are referring to how the sentences in the paragraph are linked to one another logically. As you learned in Lesson 4, you might organize the sentences in a paragraph according to chronological or sequential order, by cause and effect, by comparison and contrast, in order of degree, or in spatial order. Here are some questions to ask yourself when checking the organization of your paragraphs.

- How are the sentences in the paragraph organized?
- Is this the most effective way to organize them?
- Are there any sentences that don't follow the organization or that just don't flow logically?

Let's use these questions to evaluate a paragraph from a paper.

Example

How are the sentences in the paragraph organized? They are organized sequentially.

Go fly a kite. Sounds easy, but what is really involved? Here's a quick how-to. To fly a kite with one line, first, stand with your back facing the wind. Then, hold up the kite by its bridle, and let some of the string out. Your kite should fly into the air if there is enough wind to carry it. As the kite begins to move away from you, tug on the string until the kite is high in the sky. Try it!

First step

Second step

Third step

Is this the most effective way to organize them? Since the paragraph is about the steps to flying a kite, it's very effective. You might use the same type of organization to explain how to do anything that has sequential steps.

Are there any sentences that don't follow the organization or that just don't flow? It all flows from step to step.

WRITING TIP

YOU CAN HELP your reader follow the organization of your paragraph by using certain words and phrases. Here is a list of words that tend to work well with each type of organization.

Chronological order	Cause and effect	Comparison	Contrast	Order of degree	Spatial order
First, second, third, and so on	So	Similarly	On the other hand	Most importantly	Next to
Then	Thus	Just as	Unlike	Foremost	Beside
Next	Therefore	Like	But	Moreover	Under
Before	As a result	Likewise	Although	Furthermore	Below
After	Because	In the same way	Instead	In addition	In front of
Later	Hence		Yet	First, second, third, and so on	Near
During	Consequently		Still		Above
When	Accordingly		On the contrary		Beyond
Until			In contrast		To the right
While			However		To the left
Meanwhile			Rather		In between
Since then					
Finally					
Lastly					
Eventually					

Here is a list of words you can use to connect ideas together.

When you want to	Try these words or phrases
Give an example	For example
	For instance
	In fact
	That is
	In other words
	In particular
	First, second, third, and so on
	Specifically
Add a thought	And
	In addition
	Also
	Furthermore
	Besides
	Again
	What's more
	In this way
Emphasize a thought	Indeed
	In fact
	As a matter of fact
	Certainly
	As you can see
	Clearly
Give credit to another point of view	Although
	Despite
	Though
	Even though
	Granted
	Of course
	To be sure
Sum up a series of ideas	In short
	In brief
	To sum up

PRACTICE ▶

3. Evaluate the organization of the following paragraph.

When you move into your first apartment, you will probably find that there are several things you used at home that you now will need to buy for yourself. In the kitchen, you will need silverware, dishes, dish towels, pot holders, pots, pans, and other cooking utensils. You will need towels, a shower curtain, a bath mat, and toiletries in your bathroom. If you plan to clean your apartment once in a while, you'll also need cleaning supplies and equipment specific to each room. In the bedroom, you are going to need sheets, blankets, and pillows. You will probably want to have a television set or stereo as well as furniture in your living room.

a. How are the sentences in the paragraph organized?

_____

_____

_____

b. Is this the most effective way to organize them? Explain why or why not.

_____

_____

_____

c. Are there any sentences that don't follow the organization or that just don't flow logically? Give examples and explain what the problem is.

_____

_____

_____

_____

_____

4. Choose a paragraph from one of your own drafts. Evaluate the paragraph's organization by answering these questions.

a. How are the sentences in the paragraph organized?

_____

_____

b. Is this the most effective way to organize them? Explain why or why not.

_____

_____

c. Are there any sentences that don't follow the organization or that just don't flow logically? Give examples and explain what the problem is.

_____

_____

_____

_____

_____

5. Use the Writing Tip that follows to evaluate the organization of one your own drafts.

WRITING TIP

One strategy for checking the organization of all the paragraphs in your paper is to outline your finished product. Here is an outline you can fill in using one of your own papers.

Thesis Statement: Your thesis statement as it is stated in your introduction

_____

_____

_____

I. Topic sentence from the first body paragraph

_____

_____

    A. Example 1 in first body paragraph that supports the topic sentence

_____

_____

    B. Example 2 in first body paragraph that supports the topic sentence

_____

_____

    C. Example 3 in first body paragraph that supports the topic sentence

_____

_____

II. Topic sentence from the second body paragraph

_____

_____

    A. Example 1 in second body paragraph that supports the topic sentence

_____

_____

    B. Example 2 in second body paragraph that supports the topic sentence

_____

_____

    C. Example 3 in second body paragraph that supports the topic sentence

_____

_____

III. Topic sentence from the third body paragraph

_____

_____

    A. Example 1 in third body paragraph that supports the topic sentence

_____

_____

    B. Example 2 in third body paragraph that supports the topic sentence

_____

_____

    C. and so on . . .

_____

_____

IV. Topic sentence from the fourth body paragraph

_____

_____

A. Example 1 in fourth body paragraph that supports the topic sentence

_____

_____

B. Example 2 in fourth body paragraph that supports the topic sentence

_____

_____

C. and so on . . .

_____

_____

_____

_____

_____

_____

Conclusion: Your take-home message as it is written in your conclusion

_____

_____

_____

_____

Editing Your Paper

LESSON SUMMARY

Have you ever heard someone talk with a strong accent? Maybe they had a British accent, a strong Southern accent, or a strong New York accent. Whatever the accent, it affected how you heard that person's message; you may have had to work harder to understand it, or been reminded of stereotypical examples of that accent and distracted from what the person had to say. When you write, your presentation—spelling, grammar, punctuation, and usage—also affects how others perceive your message. If your presentation is hard to understand, others have problems reading what you write. That's why it's important to edit your paper for proper spelling, grammar, punctuation, and usage.

o far, in this section you've learned how to evaluate your paper for its content and structure. In this lesson, you will look at the individual sentences and words in your paper.

▶ SPELLING CORRECTLY

Spelling does make a difference. Your teacher will probably take off points for misspelled words. More importantly, spelling affects the way your reader perceives you and your message. For example, a writer who consistently misspells words doesn't seem very careful, and the reader might start to wonder how carefully the writer checked the other facts in the paper. Fortunately, you don't have to know how to spell every word in the English language. Two great tools to help you spell correctly are:

- a computer spell checker
- a dictionary

THE COMPUTER SPELL CHECKER

Although this feature in your word processing software is a handy tool, you need to be careful when relying on it. Often, the spell checker will not recognize certain words, such as names, abbreviations, or terms that you have defined in your paper, and it will tell you they are misspelled. Also, some words that sound alike are spelled differently. If the word exists in the spell checker's dictionary, the spell checker will not catch that the word is misspelled in the context you're using it. For example, a spell checker will usually miss this misspelled word: The ball broke my window *pain*. Although *pain* is a word, it's not spelled correctly here. It should be *pane*. So use your head when making changes suggested by a spell checker. Don't allow the spell checker to automatically fix the spelling in your paper. You will have to go through your paper word-by-word with the spell checker to determine which words really are spelled incorrectly. Finally, use a dictionary as your backup.

DICTIONARIES

Any time you are unsure about the spelling of a word, you should use a dictionary to check its spelling. Use a reputable college dictionary to check your work. There are also many online dictionaries you can use if you have access to the Internet.

TEST TAKING TIP

Words that sound alike don't just fool computers. They are also a source of spelling mistakes in many students' papers. Becoming familiar with this list of words that are often confused can help you avoid some common spelling mistakes.

Words That Are Often Confused

Already means "previously."	*All ready* means "completely ready or everyone's ready."
I had already eaten dinner.	Let me know when you are all ready.
Altogether means "entirely."	*All together* means "everyone in the same place."
Mother doesn't altogether approve of my fiancé.	The family was all together last Thanksgiving.
Brake means "to slow down or stop." I may not have had the accident if I had braked sooner.	*Break* means "to fracture or shatter." Children playing at unsafe playgrounds are more likely to break bones.
A *capital* is a city. It can also refer to value, money, or accumulated goods in business, as in the word *capitalism*. Albany is the capital of New York. *Capital* can also mean something that is important or that is punishable by death. Rape is a capital crime. John proposed a capital idea!	A *capitol* is a building. The capitol in Texas is modeled on the capitol in Washington, DC. The capitol faces Congress Avenue.
Everyday means "ordinary or usual." Soon we were back to our everyday routine.	*Every day* means "each day." I walk my dog Johnson every day.

Complement means "to complete or make perfect." Mary and Philip complement one another well.	Compliment means "to say something nice about something." Philip complimented Mary on her new dress.
A *desert* is "a very dry region." I didn't realize there were so many blooming cactuses in the desert.	A *dessert* is "a sweet end to a meal." We had ice cream for dessert.
Its means "belonging to it." India is proud of its heritage.	*It's* means "it is." It's raining outside.
Lead means "to guide or go first." We want a president who can lead us to victory. *Lead* also is the name of a metal. The pipes in the building were made of lead.	*Led* means "guided, directed, or to have gone first." It is the past tense of the verb *to lead*. He led us to victory. The choir director led us in a verse of the "This Land is Our Land."
Loose means "free." My dog got loose and ran into the street.	*Lose* means "to misplace." Try not to lose your money this time.
Miner means "someone who works in a mine." A miner's job can be very dangerous.	*Minor* is "someone who is underage or less important." We do not sell cigarettes to minors.
Passed is a verb. He passed me just before I crossed the finish line.	*Past* can be a noun, adjective, or a preposition. She drove past (preposition) the bank before she realized it. It's important to remember the past (noun). Past (adjective) performance is often used to predict future performance.
Peace means "tranquility or calm." Peace is always better than war.	*Piece* means a "part." She cut the fabric into several pieces.
Personal means "individual." You might not want to discuss your personal problems at work.	*Personnel* means "employees." The personnel at my company are mostly young and enthusiastic.
Plain means "common or clear." She wore a plain suit to the wedding. *Plain* can also mean a flat piece of land. Please tell me again in plain English. Buffalo used to live on the plains.	*Plane* refers to "a carpenter's tool, an airplane, or a flat surface." The plane landed on time.
Principal means "head of a school or important." The principal reason I went to France was to learn French. The boys were sent to the principal's office.	*Principle* means "a rule." He studied the principles of accounting for two years before becoming a bookkeeper. I don't lend money to friends as a matter of principle.
Quiet means "still or silent." Please be quiet so I can hear the movie.	*Quite* means "very or completely." We are quite happy with Hannah's new school.
Threw is a verb. The pitcher threw the ball to first base.	*Through* is a preposition. The kids threw the ball through the window.
Waist means "the middle part of the body." The dress was gathered around the waist.	*Waste* means "garbage or left-over materials." Put those papers in the waste basket. *Waste* also means "to use carelessly." He's always wasting money that could be spent on a new car.
Weak means "not strong." They served very weak tea at the reception.	*Week* means "a period of seven days." Let's meet in two weeks.
Who's means "who is or who has." Who's knocking on the door? Who's been eating my candy?	*Whose* means "belonging to who." Whose paper is this?
You're means "you are." You're my best friend. You're dead wrong.	*Your* means "belonging to you." Where is your friend? Did you leave your coat at home?

PRACTICE ▶

Circle the correct word to complete each sentence.

1. When (your/you're) done with your work, let's go out to dinner.
2. If the kids would just be (quiet/quite), I think I could finish this report.
3. They walked (passed/past) the accident without realizing it.
4. My energy (complements/compliments) his calmness.
5. They went camping in the (desert/dessert).
6. The dog licked (it's/its) wounds.
7. We visited the (capital/capitol) while we were in Washington, D.C.
8. I had (already/all ready) seen the movie twice.
9. I try not to (waist/waste) money on vending machines.
10. The (principal/principle) cause of the fire was faulty wiring.
11. (Who's/Whose) house is this anyway?
12. After having the flu, Martha felt very (weak/week).

Here are a few triplets that are easily confused. Make sure you don't make these mistakes in your writing.

More Words That Are Often Confused

Scent means "smell or odor." The animal could smell our scent.	*Cent* means "one penny." I wouldn't pay a cent for that!	*Sent* means "transmitted." I sent the e-mail message two hours ago.
Sight means "ability to see." Her sight is failing. *Sight* can also mean "to spot" If you sight my missing cat, please call me immediately.	*Cite* means "to quote or reference." It's important to cite your sources in a research paper.	*Site* means "location." For more information, go to our website. We had a picnic on the site of our future house.
Right means "correct." The teacher doesn't count off points if you get the right answer.	*Write* means "to put down in writing or to record." Write your name on the top line.	*Rite* means "a ceremony or ritual." The priest performed the last rites on the victims.
There means "in or at that place." I left my jacket over there.	*Their* means "belonging to them." We went to their house.	*They're* means "they are." I don't think they're here.
To is a preposition. Let's go to the zoo.	*Too* means "also." I'm a fan of the Yankees, too. *Too* can also mean "excessively." I am too tall to fit into that dress.	*Two* comes after one and before three. I'll have two cookies please.
Where refers to a location. Where did you get that terrific hat?	*Wear* means "to put on." I hate to wear a tuxedo.	*Were* is the past tense of to be. We were much younger in 1985.

> ## PRACTICE ▶
>
> Circle the correct word to complete each sentence.
>
> **13.** They had a party at the construction (site/sight/cite).
> **14.** I'd rather do math problems than (right/write/rite) a paper.
> **15.** (There/Their/They're) seems to be a problem with the lock on this door.
> **16.** When I was younger, I liked to (where/wear/were) make-up.

▶ USING CORRECT GRAMMAR

As you've probably learned in your English classes over the years, grammar refers to how sentences are written. Like poor spelling, poor grammar can doom an otherwise very good paper. It gives your reader a bad impression and takes away from your credibility. Teachers usually penalize papers that contain poor grammar. Standardized tests often test basic grammar rules, too. So, it's very important to know what good grammar is and to use it properly when you write.

> **THINK ABOUT IT**
>
> **There are many grammar rules. Fortunately, you are already familiar with most of the rules of grammar you need to know. In fact, you probably remember carrying around a thick grammar book at some point in school. As you can tell, this book is not that thick, and it cannot cover all the rules of grammar that are important to writing. If you feel that you need to review more grammar than this book covers, get a basic English grammar workbook at your local library or school bookstore or take a basic grammar refresher course at your community college. *Grammar Essentials 2nd edition* by Judith Olsen (LearningExpress, 2000) is one title which may be helpful.**

As you probably know, a complete sentence is one that has a subject (a doer) and a verb (an action). Because we can think so much faster than we can write, sometimes we write incomplete sentences or long sentences that run on and on. These are two grammar problems you should avoid in your papers.

- Sentence fragments—incomplete sentences that lack either a subject or a verb or both
- Run-on sentences—two or more sentences that are written as one sentence

CORRECTING SENTENCE FRAGMENTS

Listed below are some of the most common errors.

Using punctuation incorrectly. Often, a fragment is caused when a writer puts a period (or other type of end punctuation) before the end of the sentence. You'll learn more about using proper punctuation in a moment.

> **Example:** You can go out with your friends. As soon as you clean your room.
> You can fix this fragment by joining the second thought to the first sentence: You can go out with your friends as soon as you clean your room.

Mistaking a list as a sentence. Sometimes, a long list of items can seem like a complete sentence. Remember, a complete sentence has a subject and a verb.

> **Example:** Having walked ten miles, gone days without food, and lost all hope.
> You can fix this fragment by joining the list to a complete sentence: Having walked ten miles, gone days without food, and lost all hope, Edgar collapsed from exhaustion.

> **Example:** Terriers, dachshunds, and poodles.
> You can fix this fragment by adding a verb: Terriers, dachshunds, and poodles are three examples of good house dogs.
> Or, you could fix it by adding a subject and a verb: Three examples of good house dogs are terriers, dachshunds, and poodles.

Mimicking spoken language. We do not always speak in complete sentences. Often, when we want our writing to sound natural and to flow smoothly, we write in a conversational style. This is OK when you are writing a dialogue and using appropriate punctuation to show that you are writing dialogue. And sometimes, professional writers will use this style of writing. However, in most of the papers you will write for school or for standardized tests, you should avoid using conversational sentence fragments.

> **Example:** Even though I didn't want to.
> You can fix this fragment by joining it to a complete sentence: I completed the assignment, even though I didn't want to.

Example: The old house down the street, which seemed like a perfect place for a ghost to live. You can fix this fragment by adding a verb: The old house down the street seemed like a perfect place for a ghost to live.

Example: Probably next week.
You can fix this fragment by adding a subject and a verb: It's probably next week.

Mistaking a phrase for a sentence. A phrase is a group of words that lacks a subject and a verb. Some phrases have verb forms that are not verbs, but are actually nouns. Sometimes, these phrases, called verbal phrases, are mistaken for complete sentences. They are not complete sentences. You can correct these fragments either by adding the verbal phrase to a complete sentence or by changing the verb form in the phrase to a real verb.

Example: Watching the sun slip behind the trees.
Let's try two ways to fix this fragment.

1. Add the verbal phrase to a complete sentence:
   Watching the sun slip behind the trees, I felt closure in my long day.
2. Change the verb form in the phrase to a real verb:
   I watched the sun slip behind the trees.

CORRECTING RUN-ON SENTENCES

Run-on sentences usually occur when the writer uses incorrect end punctuation. The writer either uses no punctuation at all to separate two or more sentences, or uses only a comma where a form of end punctuation is really needed. Here are some examples:

- You don't need to worry about me, I can take care of myself.
- The flames are out the house is no longer on fire.

Here are some ways to fix a run-on sentence.

Separate the two sentences with a period.

Example: You don't need to worry about me. I can take care of myself.

Example: The flames are out. The house is no longer on fire.

Separate the two sentences with a comma and a conjunction, such as *and, or, nor, but, for, so, yet.*

Example: The flames are out, and the house is no longer on fire.

Separate the two sentences with a semicolon.

Example: You don't need to worry about me; I can take care of myself.

Example: The flames are out; the house is no longer on fire.

Separate the two sentences with a long dash (called an em-dash).

Example: The flames are out—the house is no longer on fire.

Change one of the two sentences into a dependent clause.

Example: You don't need to worry about me because I can take care of myself.

> **THINK ABOUT IT**
>
> Notice that each corrected version of the run-on sentence actually means something a little different. When correcting a run-on sentence, think about what you want the sentence to say. Then, choose the best way to fix it to keep your intended meaning.

PRACTICE ▶

17. Correct these sentence fragments and run-on sentences.
  a. Look at the facilities in other countries have you'll see the U. S. has far better facilities.

  _____

  _____

  b. Contributing time, money, and effort.

  _____

  _____

  c. My father isn't sick, he's as healthy as a horse.

  _____

  _____

d. Having stayed up all night working on my paper.

_____

_____

e. Must be prepared and on time.

_____

_____

18. Rewrite the following paragraph. Eliminate any sentence fragments or run-on sentences.

> A person who is interested in becoming a teacher. A profession that is in great need of talented people. Should investigate the elements required to be a good teacher before making a final decision. On first thought, it might seem that a good teacher is one who is very knowledgeable of the subject matter, a master of what he or she wants to teach, however others would disagree. Good teachers are those who connect with students and are able to interest students in the process of thinking and inquiring about the subject matter. Teaching is more than knowing the subject matter it's understanding where students are and dreaming about where they can go with the subject matter.

_____

_____

_____

_____

_____

_____

_____

_____

_____

_____

_____

_____

_____

USING CORRECT PUNCTUATION

Although it may sometimes seem trivial, punctuation can really make a difference in what your paper says. Look at the following examples.

Don't! Stop now!

Don't stop now.

In the first sentence, the person is saying, "stop now!" In the second sentence, the person is saying, "now isn't a good time to stop."

Here are some tips on when to use different punctuation marks in your writing.

If Your Purpose Is To:	Use This Punctuation:	Example:
end a sentence	**period** [.]	Use a period to end a sentence.
connect complete sentences	**semicolon** [;] or a **comma** [,] *and* a **conjunction** [and, or, nor, for, so, but, yet]	A semi-colon can connect two sentences; it is an excellent way to show that two ideas are related.
connect items in a list	**comma** [,] but if one or more items in that list already has a comma, use a **semicolon** [;]	The table was overturned, the mattress was torn apart, and the dresser drawers were strewn all over the floor. The castaways included a professor, who was the group's leader; an actress; and a housewife.
introduce a quotation or explanation	**colon** [:] or **comma** [,]	Colons have three functions: introducing long lists, introducing quotations, and introducing explanations. He said, "This simply won't do."
indicate a quotation	**quotation marks** [" "]	"To be or not to be?" is one of the most famous lines from *Hamlet*.
indicate a question	**question mark** [?]	Why are so many engineering students obsessed with *Star Trek*?
connect two words that work together	**hyphen** [-]	brother-in-law, well-known author
separate a word or phrase for emphasis	**em-dash** [—]	I never lie—never.
separate a word or phrase that is relevant but not essential information	**parenthesis** [( )]	There is an exception to every rule (including this one).
show possession or contraction	**apostrophe** [']	That's Jane's car.

CAPITALIZING THE RIGHT WORDS

Here are some basic guidelines for capitalizing words.

- **Capitalize the first word of a sentence:** A sentence always begins with a capital letter.
- **Capitalize *I*** (including *I'm*, *I've*, *I'd*, and other contractions with *I*): When I started the paper, I thought I'd never finish it.
- **Capitalize the first word in a quotation that is a complete sentence.** If you are quoting only a phrase or part of a sentence, you don't need to capitalize the first word of the material you are quoting: John called out, "Hey, please stop your car!" Then, he praised the man in the car for being "the most polite driver" he'd ever met.
- **Capitalize the first and last words and all words that are not articles in the titles of movies, songs, works of art, and written materials:** *To Kill a Mockingbird, A Farewell to Arms, A Field Guide to Spiders and Scorpions of Texas*
- **Capitalize proper nouns and proper adjectives.** If you're not sure what counts as a proper noun or a proper adjective, examples of these are listed below.

PROPER NOUNS AND PROPER ADJECTIVES	EXAMPLES
People's names	Marianne Jones, John F. Kennedy, Jr., Georgianne O'Reilly
Names of places	Coney Island, New York City, North America, Rocky Mountains, Central Park, Empire State Building, Lincoln Memorial
Names of businesses, organizations, and other institutions	German Club, Southern Methodist University, House of Representatives, National Geographic Society
Names of historical events	Civil War, Korean War, American Revolution

Things you find on a calendar	Monday, June, Halloween, Memorial Day, Independence Day, Mother's Day
Names of nationalities, races, and religions	African-American, Roman Catholic, French, Canadian
People's titles	Dean Chang, President Johnson, Chief Justice, Aunt Mary, Cousin John

PRACTICE ▶

19. Rewrite the following paragraph using correct punctuation and capitalization.

> Several months ago february 29 I had just watched the ending of a very funny movie i reached over, turned off the TV and was just beginning to dream quite pleasantly when the familiar ring of my telephone suddenly startled me awake groggily I answered my telephone it was my best friend telling me he had just been given extra tickets to the yankees game he excitedly asked would you like to go

_____

_____

_____

_____

_____

_____

_____

_____

_____

_____

_____

_____

_____

_____

▶ USING WORDS CORRECTLY

The writing problems discussed in the following pages are often called *usage* problems. They have to do with using words correctly. Read through this list of often misused words and note any that apply to you.

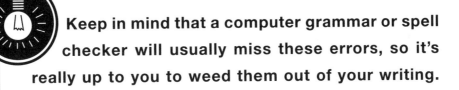

Accept means "to receive"

Except means "to leave out or exclude"

Examples:

> I accept your apology.
>
> I can meet with you any day except Fridays.

Adapt means "to change so one fits in better"

Adopt means "to make something one's own"

Examples:

> When our trip to the zoo was suddenly cancelled, we adapted our plans.
>
> We adopted the stray dog.

Affect means "to influence"

Effect as a verb means "to make happen"

Effect as a noun means "the result of something"

Examples:

> Don't let your neighbor's business affect you.
>
> The court effected a mandatory waiting period.
>
> The effects of the explosion were apparent.

Bad is an adjective. It should be used to modify nouns and pronouns.

Badly is an adverb. It should be used to modify verbs, adjectives, and adverbs.

Examples:

> I feel bad about what happened.
>
> We had a really bad day.
>
> Our band played badly last night.

Discover means "to find something that already existed but was not known"

Invent means "to make something new that didn't exist before"

Examples:

> The scientists discovered a new species of cave salamander.
>
> Eli Whitney invented the cotton gin.

Emigrate means "to leave one's country to live somewhere else"

Immigrate means "to come to a new country to live"

Examples:

> The political unrest caused many people to emigrate to new countries.
>
> John's family immigrated to the United States three generations ago.

Fewer is used before plural nouns

Less is used before nouns that do not have a plural form. Do not use *less* in front of plural nouns.

Examples:

> Incorrect: I have less days to prepare for the exam than I thought I had.
>
> Correct: I have fewer days to prepare for the exam than I thought I had.
>
> Correct: I have less money than I did before Christmas.

Imply means "to suggest something that isn't said explicitly"

Infer means "to deduce"

Examples:

> John implied at dinner that he might want to see other girls.
>
> I inferred from our dinner conversation that John might break up with me soon.

Lie means "to recline"

Lay means "to put"

These verbs have similar past forms, so we sometimes confuse them. The following chart outlines their forms.

Verb	Present participle	Past	Past Participle
to lie (recline)	(is) lying	lay	(have) lain
to lay (put)	(is) laying	laid	(have) laid

Examples:

> You should lie down if you feel sick.
>
> She wasn't feeling well, so she lay down for an hour.
>
> She had just lain down when the guests arrived.
>
> She had just laid the baby down when the guests arrived.
>
> I left my homework laying on the dining room table.
>
> Marsha always leaves her clothes laying on the floor beside the bed.

Persecute means "to attack"

Prosecute means "to bring legal action against"

Examples:

> Those who do not agree with the current political regime are persecuted daily.
>
> It's our store policy to prosecute those who shoplift.

Rise means "to go up"

Raise means "to move something up"

These verbs have similar past forms, so we sometimes confuse them. The following chart outlines their forms.

Verb	Present participle	Past	Past Participle
to rise	(is) rising	rose	(have) risen
to raise	(is) raising	raised	(have) raised

Examples:

The stock market has risen three days in a row now.

The post office has raised stamp prices twice in the past two years.

Sit means "to rest or get into a sitting position"

Set means "to put or place"

Examples:

Please sit down and rest a moment before leaving.

Please set those heavy books down and take a rest.

Than is a conjunction

Then is an adverb and means "at that time or next"

Examples:

I am taller than Estrella.

We then sat down to a good meal.

PRACTICE ▶

Circle the correct word to complete each sentence.

20. (Fewer/Less) people are killed in airplane accidents each year (than/then) in car accidents.

21. In the novel, two Martians (emigrated/immigrated) from Mars to Earth.

22. Do you know who (discovered/invented) the telephone?

23. He (accepted/excepted) my apology graciously.

24. We (implied/inferred) from her tone of voice that we were in trouble.

25. A cat is usually slow to (adapt/adopt) to a new cat in the house.

26. Did the flood (effect/affect) your house?

27. As a child, he played the violin (bad/badly).

28. The Valentine's candy (lay/laid) unopened on her dresser.

29. The puppy is (lying/laying) down in the grass outside.

30. (Set/Sit) your keys down on the desk and come in.

WRITING TIP

Use this Editing Checklist when you edit your paper.

_____ Is the spelling correct? Did you use the spell check on the computer or look up words you weren't sure about in a dictionary?

_____ Is the grammar correct? Are there any sentence fragments or run-on sentences?

_____ Have you used punctuation correctly?

_____ Have you correctly used capital letters?

_____ Have you used words correctly throughout the paper?

Being Clear and Concise

LESSON SUMMARY

Have you ever met a person who used very sophisticated vocabulary? Perhaps you and others had a hard time even following what this person was saying. Or, maybe you understood him fine, but were totally turned off by his pretentious style. It's the same with writing papers. In this lesson, you will learn some ways to make sure your writing is clear and concise, so others can follow your message and not be turned off by a complex style.

One of the most important things you need to know about writing is to make it simple and clear. In this lesson, you will learn techniques that will help you become the kind of writer who can discuss ideas that can quickly and easily be understood by others.

▶ WRITING CLEAR SENTENCES

There are three main strategies for keeping your sentences clear.

- Be brief.
- Use the active voice.
- Avoid unnecessarily "big" words.

Often when you are given a writing assignment, it will have a minimum word limit. So you may think, "The more words I use, the faster I get to the end of the assignment." This is usually not the best guarantee for a good grade. If you have brainstormed and researched your topic, you'll find you have plenty of information to work with. And it's important to remember that writing assignments are not about counting words, so much as what those words have to say.

▶ How to Be Concise

When writing sentences, try to choose your words carefully. Unnecessary words clutter up your sentences, cover up your meaning, and often frustrate your reader. Here are some ways to say what you really want to say.

Get rid of *that, who,* and *which* when you can.

INSTEAD OF WRITING	TRY
It was a trip *that was very memorable.*	It was *a memorable trip.*
She wished *that* she had taken the job offer *that* she had been given more seriously.	She wished she had taken the job offer more seriously.
Let's eat in the restaurant *that is air conditioned.*	Let's eat in the *air-conditioned* restaurant.
My neighbor, *who is the president of the PTA,* has six children.	My neighbor, *the president of the PTA,* has six children.
The building next door, *which used to be abandoned,* is now a community center for kids after school.	The building next door, *once abandoned,* is now a community center for kids after school.
Anyone who is pregnant should avoid roller coasters.	*Pregnant women* should avoid roller coasters.

Try to avoid using *there is* and *it is*.

INSTEAD OF WRITING	TRY
It was with great regret that I fired my secretary.	*Regrettably,* I fired my secretary.
There is no reason for the department to pursue a criminal investigation.	*The department has no reason* to pursue a criminal investigation.

Avoid using *I believe, I feel, I think, I am of the opinion that,* and *in my opinion.*

INSTEAD OF WRITING	TRY
I am of the opinion that circuses are cruel to animals.	Circuses are cruel to animals.
I believe that violent crimes should be punished severely.	Violent crimes should be punished severely.
I am of the opinion that mothers should be able to breastfeed in public.	Mothers should be able to breastfeed in public.

Use prepositional phrases when they are appropriate.

INSTEAD OF WRITING	TRY
When you come to the second stop sign, turn right.	*At the second stop sign,* turn right.
While we were at the dinner party, an allergy attack caused him to sneeze.	*During the dinner party,* an allergy attack caused him to sneeze.

Replace *so* and *so that* with infinitive phrases (*to + verb*).

INSTEAD OF WRITING	TRY
I want to smell the *fish so that I am sure it's fresh.*	I want to smell the fish *to make sure it's fresh.*
Close the windows *so that the air conditioning stays inside the house.*	Close the windows *to keep the air conditioning inside the house.*

Replace *because of the fact that* with *because.*

INSTEAD OF WRITING	TRY
Because of the fact that Manny realizes he doesn't want to be like Lenny, he finally feels at peace with himself at the end of the novel.	*Because* Manny realizes he doesn't want to be like Lenny, he finally feels at peace with himself at the end of the novel.
Because of the fact that I love you, I know we will always stay together.	*Because I love you,* I know we will always stay together.

▶ How to Use the Active Voice

When you use the active voice, you tell *who is doing something.* For example, Mitch hit the ball. In this sentence, you know that Mitch did the hitting. Now compare this sentence with the following one: The ball was hit. In this sentence, you don't know who hit the ball. Of course, you can always change the sentence to read: The ball was hit by Mitch. But compare these two sentences:

- Mitch hit the ball. (Active voice)
- The ball was hit by Mitch. (Passive voice)

The first sentence sounds interesting. It's clear, easy to follow, and briefer than the second sentence. The second sentence is in the passive voice. In general, you should try to write in the active voice.

Of course, there are exceptions to this rule. If you don't know who is doing the action, a passive sentence makes more sense. Also, if you want to emphasize the action and not the person doing the action, you might use a passive sentence. Here are some examples.

- Our dog was hit by a car.
- José was showered with money.
- Margaret was overwhelmed with sadness.

▶ How to Weed Out Words or Phrases that Get in the Way of Your Meaning

When you write, try to avoid words that your reader is unlikely to know. To be a "big" word, a word doesn't have to be long; it just has to prevent you from getting your message across. Here are some "big" words to avoid:

- **Abbreviations and acronyms**—shortened forms of words represented by capital letters
- **Jargon**—words that are used in specific ways in different fields
- **Pretentious words**—showy words, especially those that aren't used properly

ABBREVIATIONS
While abbreviations can certainly be helpful, your reader won't have a clue what you're trying to say if he or she isn't familiar with the term you are using in your writing.

- *Because the dog had AKC papers, he was worth a lot more money than we anticipated.*
  If your audience doesn't know that AKC stands for American Kennel Club, you've lost them. Even if your reader knows what AKC stands for, they still may not know what this sentence means.

- *In light of the spread of AIDS, traditional STDs are no longer the focus of sex education classes that they once were.*

  You can probably assume that your audience is familiar with the term *AIDS*. But unless they are in the fields of public health or biology, they aren't likely to know that STD stands for sexually-transmitted disease. You might even go so far as to give examples of what these diseases are, so your audience understands your point.

ACRONYMS

An acronym is a word that is formed from the first letters or parts of a series of words. For example, AIDS (*acquired immune deficiency syndrome*), radar (*radio detecting and ranging*), and scuba (*self-contained underwater breathing apparatus*) are common acronyms.

- *When buying a new computer, make sure to get one with enough RAM* (random access memory).

  What is RAM? If your audience isn't familiar with computers, you'll lose them.

JARGON

Jargon consists of technical or specialized terms used in specific fields. If your audience isn't in the field, you'll probably lose them. It's best to avoid jargon as much as possible. When you do use jargon, make sure to define the terms so your reader can follow your message. Otherwise, you're just wasting your time.

- *You don't have any PIP coverage, so there is no medical coverage for your driving into that tree.*

  If your insurance agent said this to you, would you know what it means? Unless you work in insurance, you probably won't know what this means. PIP stands for Personal Injury Protection. It's the part of an insurance policy that pays when a person is injured in a car accident.
- *Do you have a LAN in the office?*

  If you don't work in IT (information technology), you probably aren't familiar with what a LAN is. LAN stands for Local Area Network. It's a configuration of several computers within a geographic area that allows for sharing of resources.

SHOWY WORDS

- *He possesses a Jaguar.*

  Why not just say: He owns a Jaguar or He has a Jaguar?
- *Have you ever utilized a sandwich maker before?*

  Why not just say: Have you ever used a sandwich maker before?

It's okay to use specific words that convey your meaning. But don't say something simple in complicated words just to use those words. Look at these examples.

- He sauntered home from school.
- He raced home from school.
- He stumbled home from school.
- He crept home from school.
- He slithered home from school.

Each of these sentences gives the reader a different picture of what happened. It wouldn't be appropriate to change any of these sentences to "He came home from school." You would lose the meaning and the image created by these other verbs.

WRITING TIP

These two tips can help you write more simply and clearly.

- **Get to the point.** Try to keep your introduction and build-up as brief as possible. Of course, you'll want the reader to have enough context to understand your message, but don't go on and on. Then, present your message in a logical way. If you are trying to explain a general rule that has some exceptions, for example, explain the rule first. Then, give the exceptions. Don't interrupt the logical flow of your ideas with exceptions or extraneous information.
- **Make your reader's job as easy as possible.** Reading takes time and effort. You want your reader focused on your message rather than on figuring out what you are saying. If your reader is working just to understand your words, he or she may misunderstand your message.

PRACTICE ▶

1. Rewrite the following paragraph using the strategies in this lesson.

A person's accomplishments in life are dependent upon his personal prediction of his performance. In actuality, anyone can effect his own future, positively or negatively, through truthful evaluation of his self-esteem. If an individual sees himself as incapable of producing anything that is of value, he is correct. Difficulties will be encountered that are overwhelming in his pursuits of success because of the fact that he is beginning with self-doubt. Although he might be qualified to accomplish a particular project, he will probably fail because of the fact that he will be easily persuaded to surrender his efforts and stop struggling toward his goal.

Writing with Style

LESSON SUMMARY

You're at a dinner party and an elegantly dressed guest arrives. All the heads in the room turn to watch this person calmly enter the room. This person has style. They may not be the most attractive or intelligent person you've ever met, but people pay attention to this person. When you write with style, your reader also pays attention. In this lesson, you will learn some tips for finding your own style.

Think of a writer you enjoy reading. Perhaps it's a newspaper columnist, a novelist, or a comic book writer. What is it about this writer you enjoy? Did you like the wit, the imagery, the energy? Something about this writer pleases you. It probably has something to do with his or her style. Good writers usually find their own style and develop it.

THINK ABOUT IT

This book can't tell you what your writing style is or what it should be. As you become a better writer, you will develop your own style—a style that feels comfortable and comes to you naturally. The tips in this lesson will show you ways to express your ideas more vividly and clearly. Try these ideas out. If they don't feel comfortable, don't force them into your writing. Only you can find your own style and it will take time and practice.

As you try to find your own style of writing, keep these three things in mind:

- Say it naturally.
- Vary your sentence structure.
- Try out different types of figurative language.

▶ SAY IT NATURALLY

You may wonder how you are supposed to write naturally after all the "rules" you've been given in this book so far. It must seem like there are a lot of constraints on writing properly. In fact, there are different levels of formality in writing just as there are in speaking. You probably already adjust the way you speak to the situation. You might say, "How are you today, Dr. Rodriguez?" to your political science professor, but "What's up, man?" to your good friend.

You might be more relaxed when you talk to your friend than when you address your professor. However, in both cases you are saying what comes naturally to you. As you become a better writer, you will become more proficient at writing naturally at different levels and for different situations. Whenever something feels very uncomfortable, rethink what you are saying and how you are saying it. See if there is a more natural way for you to express your message for the audience.

▶ VARY YOUR SENTENCE STRUCTURE

Sometimes writers use a similar sentence structure to emphasize a point or to get the reader's attention. However, using similar sentence structures over and over again in a paper bores your reader. In fact, it makes it hard to pay attention, because the sentences do not flow. Read the following paragraph for an example.

Example

> Falls are common in homes. They can cause injuries. They occur in bathrooms. They occur in the kitchen. They occur on stairs. They can be prevented by cleaning up spills quickly and using a step stool when you need to reach something in a high place. They can also be prevented by using only non-slip rugs and removing items on stairways that could cause you to trip.

Now compare it to this version.

> Falls are common in homes. They can cause injuries. Often, falls occur in bathrooms, in the kitchen, or on stairs. You can prevent falls by cleaning up spills quickly and using a step stool when you need to reach something in a high place. It's also important to use only non-slip rugs and to remove items that you could trip on from stairs.

Which version of the paragraph was easier to read? Which one was more interesting? Which one did you want to keep reading? To keep your reader interested, try these tips:

- Use questions and answers.
- Vary the length of your sentences.
- Use different sentence structures.

Let's see these tips at work. First, read this letter to the editor of a newspaper.

Example

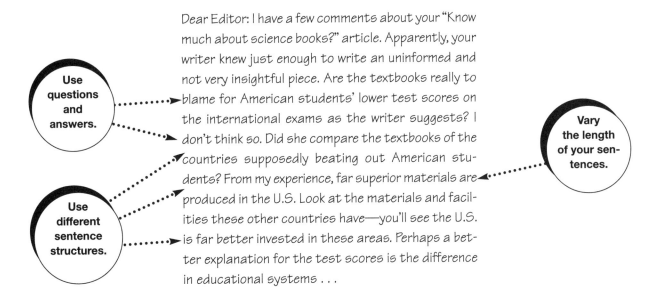

Dear Editor: I have a few comments about your "Know much about science books?" article. I think your writer wrote an uninformed and not very insightful piece. I don't think the textbooks are to blame for American students' lower test scores on the national exams. I don't think the writer compared the textbooks in different countries with those in the U.S. I think that far superior materials are produced in the U.S. I think the U.S. is far better invested in these areas. I think a better explanation for the lower test scores may be the difference in educational systems . . .

> Avoid using the same sentence structure over and over.

Now compare it to this letter.

> Use questions and answers.

> Use different sentence structures.

Dear Editor: I have a few comments about your "Know much about science books?" article. Apparently, your writer knew just enough to write an uninformed and not very insightful piece. Are the textbooks really to blame for American students' lower test scores on the international exams as the writer suggests? I don't think so. Did she compare the textbooks of the countries supposedly beating out American students? From my experience, far superior materials are produced in the U.S. Look at the materials and facilities these other countries have—you'll see the U.S. is far better invested in these areas. Perhaps a better explanation for the test scores is the difference in educational systems . . .

> Vary the length of your sentences.

PRACTICE ▶

1. Rewrite the following paragraph using questions and answers, different sentence lengths and different sentence structures.

> Henri Henklebeck is my best friend. He called last Sunday. He asked if I'd heard the news of the circus coming to town. He talked to me for a long time. We decided to spend the afternoon at the circus. We said good-bye.

_____

_____

_____

_____

_____

_____

_____

_____

_____

_____

▶ TRY SOME FIGURATIVE LANGUAGE

Figurative language is a different way of expressing ideas. You've probably used it yourself when speaking to others or when writing papers. It can bring a fresh way of looking at something or a vivid image to your reader's mind. In fact, most authors use figures of speech or figurative language because it makes the ideas and images they talk about much easier for the reader to picture. The most common are similes and metaphors. Here are some examples.

- "I jumped up and down and cried like a whole bucketful of tears." (Simile)
- "Papa's words perked me up just like air does a deflated inner tube." (Simile)
  Where the Red Fern Grows by Wilson Rawls
- "With all the things I had learned—in all the languages I had mastered—all I could say to her, standing on the porch staring at me, was, "Maaaa." Like a dry-mouthed lamb at the udder." (Simile)
  Flowers for Algernon by Daniel Keyes
- "Hold fast to dreams
  For if dreams die
  Life is a broken-winged bird
  That cannot fly." (Metaphor)
  "Dreams" by Langston Hughes

- "From the day Mr. Radley took Arthur home, people said the house died." (Personification)
- "Lightning rods guarding some graves denoted dead who rested uneasily; stumps of burned-out candles stood at the heads of infant graves. It was a happy cemetery." (Irony)
  To Kill a Mockingbird by Harper Lee
- "I'd rather have been dragged across a cactus desert and dropped thirsty in a lake of salt than listen to him. . . . " (Hyperbole)
- "The roses only sighed a moment before the sun sucked even that little breather away." (Personification)
  Parrot in the Oven by Victor Martinez

THINK ABOUT IT

You may be thinking, "Wait a minute! Isn't this the opposite of what you've been telling me in this book? I thought I was supposed to use as few words as possible and write in simple, direct language." If you're thinking this, then you've been paying attention.

It's true, you should write concisely, simply and directly because it makes your reader's job easier. However, when writing fiction and poetry, figurative language can make your reader's job very enjoyable. Creating pictures with your words allows them to take shape and form, and they appear as special features or movies for an audience of readers.

Forms of figurative language are simply tools that you can use as a writer. They may not be appropriate to every paper you write, and they may not appeal to every audience. You may not even feel comfortable using figurative language, but you should know that you can use different types of figurative language in your writing, just as other effective writers do.

This list of figurative language and definitions may be helpful as you write.

Types of Figurative Language

Metaphor—a comparison in which one thing is described as if it were something else

Simile—a comparison in which one thing is described using the word *like* or *as*

Personification—writing about a nonhuman thing as if it were human

Hyperbole—a huge exaggeration

Irony—creates a contrast between what is said or written and what is really meant

PRACTICE ▶

2. Write one sentence using each type of figurative language listed below.

 a. Metaphor

 _____

 _____

 _____

 b. Simile

 _____

 _____

 _____

 c. Personification

 _____

 _____

 _____

 d. Hyperbole

 _____

 _____

 _____

 e. Irony

 _____

 _____

 _____

Special Writing Situations

Essay Exams

LESSON SUMMARY

Does the thought of an essay exam make your palms sweat, your heart beat fast, and your stomach upset? This lesson will show you how to take an essay exam without fear. You'll learn a step-by-step approach to tackling any essay exam.

The best thing you can do to prepare for an essay exam is to think about the purpose of the exam, and the purpose of many essay exams is to test whether you have learned the material or not. These are the types of exams you are likely to have in your science, history, or psychology classes. For these exams, you will need to focus on the material you learned in class and in your textbook. In a composition class, the purpose of an essay exam will be to test your writing skills. For this kind of essay, you should put more emphasis on the form and style of your writing.

> Here are some types of essay exams you will probably encounter while in school.
>
> ▶ The questions on a literature essay exam will test whether you have read and thought about the reading assignments in the class. They might ask if you can relate the different aspects of the reading assignments to each other or to your life. Or, you

might be asked if you can interpret the plot and the characters' actions.

- The questions on a science essay exam will test whether you have learned certain facts and understand certain processes. Can you list relevant facts objectively? Can you draw conclusions from given facts?
- The essays on a history essay exam will expect you to recall events and dates and interpret them. What happened when? Why does it matter? What did it lead to?

Although the quality of your writing is always important on an essay exam, it can't save you if you haven't studied the material covered on the exam. Knowing the material will give you something to write about. Without that knowledge, it will be hard to answer the questions. The main job in preparing for an essay exam in many of your classes will have more to do with learning the material than with writing.

▶ STARTING THE TEST

Before you ever start writing your response to an essay question, you need to do these things:

- **Read over the entire test.** Read the directions carefully, and preview all the questions on the test. Start thinking about which question you will answer first. It's a good idea to start with questions that are worth the most points or questions that seem the easiest for you to answer. Don't panic if you don't immediately know all the answers. As you go through the test and as you do the next few steps, the answers will probably come to you—if you are prepared for the test.
- **Budget the time you have for the test according to the questions.** For example, you might want to give more time to questions worth more points. You'll want to make sure you have time to answer all of the questions.
- **Break down each question.** Look for the direction words. A helpful list of these words is in Lesson 1.

Example: Assume you come across the following essay question on a biology exam: *Compare and contrast aerobic exercise and resistance exercise. What are the benefits of each kind of exercise? Give examples of each kind of exercise.*

What do you need to do to answer this question?
- Tell how aerobic exercise and resistance exercise are alike and different
- Tell the benefits of aerobic exercise and resistance exercise

- Give examples of aerobic exercises and resistance exercises

- **Start thinking about your responses.** You might jot down your ideas about each question or sketch a quick outline on scratch paper. Plan your answers wisely because you will probably have little or even no time to revise your essays. Make sure you address each part of each question.

Example: Let's assume that you studied aerobic exercise and resistance exercise in your biology class. In fact, there is a section in your textbook about these two kinds of exercises. Based on your study, you might jot down the following notes.

Aerobic—jogging, swimming, cycling
- Improves body's ability to use oxygen
- Helps heart pump more efficiently
- Leads to greater endurance

Resistance—weight-lifting, chin ups, push ups
- Increases strength
- Does not increase body's endurance

PRACTICE ▶

Use the following excerpt from a business textbook to answer the questions that follow.

The Americans with Disabilities Act
On July 26, 1990, President Bush signed the Americans with Disabilities Act (ADA) into law. One of the principal aims of the ADA is to extend the civil rights protection provided to groups based on race, color, national origin, sex, and religion to the more than 43 million American citizens with disabilities. The protection provided in the ADA aims to increase the wage rate and the employment rate of disabled individuals by eliminating employer discrimination.

Definitions of the ADA's Terms
Title I of the ADA prohibits employers from discriminating against qualified individuals with disabilities. It requires covered employers to provide reasonable accommodation to the known mental or physical limitations of a qualified person with a disability, unless doing so would create an undue hardship on the employer. The meaning of the basic terms used to define Title I of the ADA are discussed below.

Employer
The term *employer* in the ADA refers to private employers, employment agencies, state and local governments, and labor organizations. Covered employers do not include the United States government, a corporation wholly owned by the United States, or a Native American tribe.

Discrimination
Discrimination includes limiting, segregating, or classifying a job applicant or employee in a way that adversely affects his or her opportunities or status based on the person's disability. The ADA specifically covers job application procedures; hiring, advancement, and discharge procedures; compensation and benefit packages; and job training.

Disability
A person with a disability is defined in the ADA as an individual who meets *one* of the following criteria: (1) has a physical or mental impairment, which may be apparent or hidden, that substantially limits one or more of the individual's major life activities, such as walking, seeing, speaking, or the ability to perform manual tasks; (2) has a record of such an impairment, such as a recovery from mental illness; *or* (3) is regarded as having such an impairment. An impairment does *not* include physical characteristics; predisposition to illness; pregnancy; personality traits that are not the result of a psychological disorder; environmental, cultural, or educational disadvantages; or advanced age.

1. Assume you come across the following essay questions on a business exam. What task does each question require you to do?

   a. What is the ADA? Who is covered by the ADA? Who is not?

   _____

   _____

   _____

   b. What does the term *disability* mean in the ADA? Give examples of who does and does not qualify as a person with a disability.

   _____

   _____

   _____

   c. What are some aims of the ADA? What kinds of processes does the ADA cover?

   _____

   _____

   _____

2. Choose one of the essay questions in 1 above. Then, use the information in the excerpt to sketch a quick outline of what you might include in your response.

   _____

   _____

   _____

   _____

   _____

   _____

   _____

   _____

   _____

   _____

▶ DRAFTING YOUR ANSWER

Now it's time to write. Most of your time should be spent on writing your essays. You know these steps already, but here they are again.

- **Write a thesis statement.** A quick way to write a thesis statement is to turn an essay question into its answer. Whatever your thesis statement, make sure it answers the question and that you can support it. Use your outline or the notes you sketched out to help you formulate a good thesis statement that you can support.

  Example: Write a possible thesis sentence for the following essay question on a biology exam: *Compare and contrast aerobic exercise and resistance exercise. What are the benefits of each kind of exercise? Give examples of each kind of exercise.* Remember, you are working on a biology essay exam, so you want to focus on objective, factual statements. You might begin with a thesis statement like this one: Both aerobic exercise and resistance exercise benefit the body.

- **Support your thesis.** Again, your outline or prewriting notes should guide your writing. If new ideas come to you as you write, include them as well.
- **Conclude your essay.** End your essay by restating your thesis statement. Add a take-home message if you have time.

PRACTICE ▶

3. Write a thesis statement for each of the following essay questions. Refer to the excerpt of the business textbook in the last practice set if you need to.

   a. What is the ADA? Who is covered by the ADA? Who is not?

   _____

   _____

   _____

   b. What does the term *disability* mean in the ADA? Give examples of who does and does not qualify as a person with a disability.

   _____

   _____

   _____

   c. What are some aims of the ADA? What kinds of processes does the ADA cover?

   _____

   _____

   _____

▶ REVIEWING YOUR ANSWERS

If you have time, you should always try to review your answers. Usually, you will not have time to write multiple drafts of your essays on a timed exam. However, you should try to do the following things.

- **Read each essay question again and make sure you have answered the question.** Check that you have answered all parts of the question, not just the first part.
- **Add any ideas that you might have forgotten the first time.** As you read, you might see ways to complement your original answer. You probably won't have time to rewrite your first essay, but you can add to it.
- **Check your essay for spelling, grammar, punctuation, and usage errors.** You can review these common errors in Lesson 10.

It's important to prepare for an essay exam. The night before the exam, you might feel the urge to stay up all night cramming facts into your head. Think twice before you do this. Staying up all night can make you tired and slow-thinking by the time of the test. Here's a better approach when preparing for an essay exam.

- Study in advance. You'll be more likely to understand the material and know how to use it in your essays.
- Get plenty of rest, especially the night before the test. You'll want to be well-rested and on your toes for the test.
- Eat a good breakfast the morning of the test. You'll need the energy for the test. You don't want to deal with a growling stomach throughout an essay exam.
- Relax. You can do it!

14 ▶ Research Papers

LESSON SUMMARY

A research paper may seem like a heavy burden to you in the beginning, but it can actually be an exciting project. It's an opportunity for you to learn about a topic you are interested in and to share the result of your research with others. In this lesson, you'll learn the basic steps to writing a research paper: finding and researching a topic, drafting your paper, and revising your paper.

Many professors will require you to write a research paper at some point during the course. As soon as you find out about the assignment, begin thinking about what you'll need to do. Often, your teacher will specify the kind of topic, the length of the paper, the format of the paper, and other details. Familiarize yourself with the instructions your teacher gives you because how you follow them will probably count as part of your final grade on the paper.

THINK ABOUT IT

School isn't the only place that will require you to write a research paper. In fact, if you look closely, you'll see research papers all around you. Pick up any newspaper or magazine—you'll probably find at least one report that involved researching a topic and distilling the information into a coherent piece. (Even news reports on the radio and television fall into the category of research reports—they're just not presented in a written form—unless you buy the transcripts.) Many jobs will require you to do these same things. So don't fret about having to write a research paper—you're actually learning some of the most useful skills you can, and you'll probably have many opportunities to apply them in the future.

▶ FINDING A RESEARCH TOPIC

Finding a topic for a research paper can be a lot of fun. Often, depending on the assignment and your teacher's instructions, you can research anything that interests you. So start thinking of a question you've been wanting to learn about: How do dolphins communicate? What is LASIK surgery? How are companies using the Internet? Can't think of anything offhand? Then try the strategies in Lesson 2.

Once you've found a topic you're interested in, make sure it's appropriate for your assignment. First, ask yourself these questions.

- Is the topic broad or narrow enough to fit into the length specified for the assignment?
- Does the topic fit the purpose of the writing assignment?
- Is the topic appropriate for your audience?
- Is the topic appropriate for a research paper?

Example: Let's say you are interested in writing a research paper on caves. That's a very broad topic—much too broad for a research paper. You will probably need to narrow the topic down to something that will fit into the length of a research paper. For example, you could write about any of the following aspects of caves:

- geology of caves—how they form
- geography of caves—where they are
- spelunking/exploring caves
- animals that inhabit caves
- human history in caves—cave people
- ancient cave art

Once you're satisfied that you've found an appropriate topic for the assignment, then go talk to your teacher. It's always a good idea to get your teacher's opinion about your topic or even to get your topic approved before you invest a lot of time researching it.

PRACTICE ▶

1. In Lesson 2 you learned about different strategies to help you come up with your own topic for a writing assignment:
   - Exploring your own areas of expertise
   - Browsing different sources for ideas
   - Keeping a clip file
   - Writing in a journal
   - Asking others for ideas
   - Gleaning ideas from your environment

   Use one of these strategies to come up with a topic you could use for a research paper.

▶ RESEARCHING YOUR TOPIC

Once you have a topic, you are ready to begin your research. Just as knowing your material is important on an essay exam, knowing your topic is important to a research paper. You cannot write about what you do not know. Here's one approach to research.

- Generate a list of research questions.
- Look for sources you can use.
- Evaluate the credibility of your sources.
- Make a list of your sources.
- Take notes from your sources.
- Organize the information you have found.

GENERATE A LIST OF RESEARCH QUESTIONS

A good way to begin researching your topic is to generate a list of questions you will research. Think of things you want to learn about your topic, why they are important, and why you want to learn them. This activity should get your creative juices flowing.

Example: Let's assume you've decided to write about cave animals. You might generate a list of research questions like these.

- What kinds of animals live in caves?
- Where in caves do animals live?
- How are cave animals different from other animals? How are animals adapted for cave life?
- What do cave animals eat?
- Are cave animals in danger of extinction?

2. Generate a list of research questions for the topic you came up with in Practice **1** on page 127.

_____

_____

_____

_____

_____

_____

_____

LOOK FOR SOURCES YOU CAN USE TO ANSWER YOUR RESEARCH QUESTIONS

Sometimes, a teacher will specify the number and kinds of sources you should include in your research. Usually, though, you will be on your own. A good place to start is your school library or local public library. There, you will find the following—and other—types of reference materials.

SOURCE	WHAT YOU'LL FIND IN IT	EXAMPLES
Almanacs and yearbooks	Statistics, facts, trivia by year (you'll need to look at the 2000 volume for information on 1999)	*The World Almanac, Facts on File*
Atlases	Maps, information about geography, including climate, rainfall, crops, population, and so on	*National Geographic Atlas, Rand McNally Atlas of the World*
Biographical dictionaries	Information about famous people	*Larousse Dictionary of Scientists, Webster's Biographical Dictionary of American Authors, African American Women: A Biographical Dictionary, Who's Who*
Dictionaries	Lists of words, their meanings, usage, history, pronunciation, and so on	*Webster's New Collegiate Dictionary, Academic Press Dictionary of Science and Technology, Harvard Dictionary of Music*
Encyclopedias	Articles on different topics	*Encyclopaedia Britannica, The World Book Encyclopedia, Encyclopedia of Mammals, Larousse Dictionary of World Folklore*
Databases	Electronic compilations of articles from periodicals and other sources	*FirstSearch, EBSCOhost*
Indexes	Lists of articles that have been published in periodicals	*Reader's Guide to Periodical Literature*

Internet	Access to websites around the world	www.cnn.com, www.time.com
Periodicals	Magazines and newspapers—articles may be found in hard copy, on microfilm or microfiche, or in electronic databases	*The New York Times, The Wall Street Journal, The New Yorker, The Science Teacher, Consumer Reports*
Quotation books	Lists of quotations arranged by author, source, keyword, subject, and so on	*Oxford Dictionary of Quotations, Bartlett's Familiar Quotations*
Vertical file	Booklets, catalogs, pamphlets, and other materials filed by subject	Individual libraries carry different levels of information in their vertical files

If you can't find what you're looking for, ask the reference librarian. These are people trained in finding specific information.

Example: What sources could you use to find the answers to your questions about the types of animals living in caves?

You might check out the following types of sources:

- encyclopedia
- nature books about caves
- ecology books
- animal field guides and encyclopedias
- magazines about exploring caves
- Internet sites
- database articles about caves and cave animals

PRACTICE ▶

3. Make a list of the types of sources you might use to find the answers to the questions you listed in question #2 above.

_____

_____

_____

_____

_____

CHECK THE CREDIBILITY OF YOUR SOURCES

When choosing sources, keep these criteria in mind.

- Is the author an authority on the subject? What are his or her credentials?

- Is the source current? In technology, science, medicine, and other fields, you will need to use the most up-to-date sources available because the information changes very quickly.
- Is the source reliable? You'll want to use sources that your audience is likely to respect. Few people are going to respect a tabloid or gossip paper, for example.

A website put up by a high school student about cave animals isn't going to carry the same weight as a paper published by a university professor who specializes in cave animals. Make sure you distinguish between sources that are credible and those that are not.

WRITING TIP

The Internet puts many, many sources at your fingertips. It's so easy to just type in a keyword and have a world of knowledge on your screen in seconds. But be careful! Everything on the Internet is not legitimate. Not every website, no matter how nicely done it is, provides information you can use for a research paper. When researching a topic, it's wise to use only websites that end in .gov (government websites), .edu (university websites, but some of these are also put up by students, so read them carefully), and sometimes .org (organizations, such as the American Cancer Society). Use your head: if information on a website seems fishy or incredible to you, verify it in another source before repeating it in your paper. Someone might call you on the information and you need to be in a position to back it up.

MAKE A LIST OF YOUR SOURCES

Once you have found sources you think you will use for your research, you should make a list of your sources. You will use the list later for your Bibliography or Works Cited list. Some people make a separate index card for each source. Others just prepare a numbered list of the sources or make a folder for each source with a photocopy of the copyright page on top. You can also use computer software that is made to specifically organize information into electronic index-type cards. However you decide to list your sources, you'll need the following information from each source:

- author's or editor's complete name
- title of the book, magazine, encyclopedia, and so on
- copyright date
- title of the article if the source is a magazine, encyclopedia, or newspaper
- data and page numbers of the article if the source is a magazine or newspaper
- publisher's name if the source is a book

WRITING TIP

Before you get too far along in your research, you might want to find out what your final paper should look like. Will you need a Works Cited list or a Bibliography? How should the entries be organized? Will you need footnotes or endnotes?

There are many different ways to format the parts of a paper. Most are explained in great detail with many examples in handbooks called style guides. Well-known style guides include *The Chicago Manual of Style, The Modern Language Association Manual of Style,* and *The American Psychological Association Manual of Style.* Usually your teacher will direct you to the style guide he or she prefers you to follow in your paper. Look at it as you prepare your list of sources—this will save you time and countless headaches later on.

Don't think that only teachers are picky about how papers are formatted. Almost all periodicals will require that you use a specific style guide and format when submitting papers for publication. Bosses are often the same way.

TAKE NOTES FROM YOUR SOURCES

As you browse your sources, you will find things you want to include in your paper. You might find quotations, statistics, or just basic information that you need to answer your research questions. You will want to record this information in a way that will be easy to find when you start writing.

Some people use an index card for each piece of information. They label the card with a number for the source, and then write the information on the card. Others take electronic notes on a laptop. Some people rely more on photocopying machines—copying the page of the source they need and highlighting the parts that interest them. Then, they include the page in a folder labeled with the source's name and other bibliographical information. Whatever method you use to take notes from your sources, be sure to label the information with the correct source name, so you can give proper credit in your paper.

ORGANIZE THE INFORMATION YOU HAVE FOUND

Go through your research notes and sort the information. Based on the information you have collected, write a tentative thesis statement of what you want to say in your research paper. (Lesson 4 gives more guidance on how to write a tentative thesis statement.) From here, you can outline your paper. Even if you don't make a formal outline, you'll need a plan for what you will write in your paper and where different pieces of your research will be used in your paper.

Example: Here's a sample outline you could use to write a research paper on cave animals.

Cave Animals

Tentative thesis statement: Although caves include animals that visit occasionally and animals that live there most of the time, true cave animals are specifically adapted for the cold, dark, moist environment of the innermost region of caves.

I. Kinds of cave animals
   A. Animals that live only in caves (troglobites)
   B. Animals that spend most of their time in caves (troglophiles)
   C. Animals that occasionally visit caves (trogloxenes)
II. Where animals live in caves—the life zones
   A. Cave entrance
      1. Cliff frogs
      2. Phoebes
   B. Twilight zone
      1. Brown crayfish
      2. Daddy-long-leg spiders
   C. Variable-temperature zone
      1. Bats
      2. Cave crickets

D. Constant-temperature zone
  1. Blind shrimp
  2. White crayfish
III. How animals are adapted to cave life
  A. Mostly invertebrates
  B. Many lack color
  C. Many are blind or eyeless

WRITING TIP

You will probably find that some of the information you thought you might include in your paper is no longer needed. Don't feel like you have to include every tidbit of your research in your paper. Stick with your thesis statement and keep your paper focused. If it's hard to toss those notes aside and forget about them, put them in your slush file. You can always use the information for a future paper.

▶ DRAFTING YOUR PAPER

Once you've completed your research and set down a tentative outline, you are ready to begin writing. You might refer to Section II for advice on drafting your paper. Here are some things to keep in mind as you write a research paper.

- Don't plagiarize.
- Cite your sources.
- Allow time for revision.

DON'T PLAGIARIZE

Plagiarism is using someone else's ideas as if they were your own. It's dishonest to present other people's ideas as your own, and it will usually get you in very serious trouble—in school, at work, everywhere. This doesn't mean you can't use your research in your paper, but you must give the credit for the ideas that are not your own and are not "common knowledge" to the source you got the information from. What is common knowledge? It's information that many have—most of the information in an encyclopedia, for example, is common knowledge. Here are four strategies for avoiding plagiarism.

- **Quote**—copy the text you want to use in your paper word-for-word and surround it with quotation marks. Then, cite the source in one of the ways described below. Be careful! You don't want your entire paper to be long quotations from other sources. Use quotations sparingly and only when they really add to your paper.
- **Paraphrase**—rewrite the main idea and the supporting details in your own words. Then, cite the source in one of the ways described below.
- **Summarize**—restate the main idea in your own words. Unlike paraphrasing, summarizing is very general. Then, cite the source in one of the ways described below.
- **Interpret**—add your own thoughts. Take the information you have collected and tell your reader what your own conclusions are. Because these are your own ideas, you do not need to cite a source for them.

CITE YOUR SOURCES

There are three main ways to give credit to your sources. Your teacher will probably tell you which way she or he prefers.

- **Footnotes.** Footnotes credit your source at the bottom of the page. They are usually numbered consecutively throughout your paper. Here are some examples (remember to follow the style guide that your teacher recommends—it may differ slightly from the one below).

Examples

[1]Culver, David C. (1982). *Cave Life: Evolution and Ecology.* Cambridge: Harvard University Press, 59.

[2]Jackman, Jack. (1997). *A Field Guide to Spiders and Scorpions of Texas.* Houston: Gulf Publishing Company, 92.

[3]Jeffrey, William R. and David P. Martasian. "Evolution and Eye Regression in Cave Fish." *American Zoologist,* Sep 1998, Vol. 38 Issue 4, 685.

- **Endnotes.** Like footnotes, endnotes are numbered consecutively throughout your paper. But they are not located on the same page as the information you are credited. Instead, you list all the credits at the end of your paper under the heading "Endnotes." Endnotes will usually look just like footnotes—they just appear at a different point in your paper.
- **Parenthetical notation.** This method allows you to credit your sources in the body of your paper. After the information you want to credit, you give the author's name and the page number in parentheses. The reader can find the actual source by going to your Works Cited or Bibliography at the end of the paper. Here's an example of what a parenthetical notation looks like (remember to follow the style guide that your teacher recommends—it may differ slightly from the one below).

Examples

(Culver 59)

(Jackman 92)

(Jeffrey 685)

ALLOW TIME FOR REVISION

Don't try to write an entire research paper in one evening. You'll want to write your paper ahead of time, so you have plenty of time away from it before you begin revising.

▶ REVISING YOUR PAPER

Refer to Section III for checklists and guidelines for revising a paper. Because research papers generally count as a major portion of a course's grade, you may choose to revise your research paper more than once.

WRITING TIP

Presentation counts. Make sure to submit your paper in a neat, typed version. Usually, research papers are typed double-spaced, with one-inch margins on all sides. If your teacher specifies a certain font or type size, be sure to follow those instructions. Typically, a research paper will contain the following parts.

- ▶ Cover sheet—includes the title of your paper, your name, the date, and any other information your teacher might request
- ▶ Outline or Table of Contents—your final outline for your paper (if you didn't do a formal outline for your paper in advance, you can always use your paper to prepare this outline)
- ▶ Body of your paper—this is the actual paper
- ▶ Endnotes—if you aren't using another method of crediting your sources
- ▶ Works Cited or Bibliography—a list of the sources you used or consulted in the course of your research

---

Writing for the Workplace

15 ▶ Business Writing

LESSON SUMMARY

What? You didn't think you'd have to write once you got out of school? Writing is actually a skill you will use throughout life. Workplace writing is perhaps one of the most important types of writing you will do after you get out of school. In this lesson, you'll learn how writing for work is different from writing for school, and how the two are similar.

"Fresh from college with a chemistry degree, I thought I had all the skills to excel in an entry-level position in the analytical chemistry lab of a pharmaceutical company. But I soon discovered that I would be spending significant time writing reports . . . ."

Lummis, Jean. "Teaching Technical Writing." *The Science Teacher,* Vol. 68 No. 7 (October 2001).

Like this person, you might be surprised to learn that writing is so important at work. But think about it for a minute: Is most of your mail from friends and family? Or, is most of your mail made up of bills, letters from businesses, and advertising inserts? If you're like most people, you get a lot of business mail. Someone at a company wrote all that stuff. In fact, workplace writing begins even before you get hired—you apply for a job with a cover letter, resume, and often an application form. And it doesn't stop there. At work, you will be expected to write e-mails, memos, business letters, reports, and even performance evaluations—if not for people you supervise, then probably for yourself. It all adds up to lots of writing at work.

► WHAT IS BUSINESS WRITING?

So far, this book has discussed writing generally—with some focus on papers you might be required to write for school. However, there are many different types of writing. For example, pull out the manual to a software program and read a paragraph. Notice how the writing in the manual is quite different from the writing you find in your local newspaper. Cookbooks, mystery novels, and poetry are all very different kinds of writing, too. Similarly, business writing has some special characteristics. Let's look at some the characteristics that make business writing different from other types of writing.

- **What?** Whether it's a proposal for a new product or a memo about your company's break room, your topic is almost always focused on some aspect of the business.
- **Who?** You might be writing to your boss, coworkers, clients, customers, or vendors—unless you are in public relations, you'll usually be writing to someone related to the business.
- **How?** Directly, briefly, clearly, purposefully—business writing is very focused and practical. Say what needs to be said as efficiently as possible so you don't waste your reader's time! To help keep business writing focused, there are a number of standard formats and styles used in business. You'll learn about several of these in the rest of this section.

► WRITING IS WRITING

Although there are some conventions specific to business writing, most of the strategies for good writing that you've learned so far in this book still apply. In business writing, you should plan what you will write before you begin writing. You can use the prewriting strategies in Section I to help you organize your thoughts. You will also probably need to draft more than one version of your letter, memo, e-mail, or report. Section II walks you through the basic steps of drafting. Finally, revising is as important to business writing as to other forms of writing. In fact, since more people will probably read your business writing and your reputation as a business person depends on it, revising is probably even more important in your business writing than it is in writing for school. Use the checklists and tips in Section III when revising your business writing.

Writing Resumes and Cover Letters

LESSON SUMMARY

Even if you don't have a job today, you still need to know something about business writing—if you ever plan to get a job. Most people's first adventure with business writing comes in the form of writing a resume and cover letter. In this lesson, you will learn the basics of resume and cover letter writing.

Before you ever start a job, you will begin practicing your business writing skills. Resumes and cover letters are key tools to getting a job. Here's what they are and how to get started writing them.

▶ WHAT IS A RESUME?

A resume is a concise, factual summary of your credentials. Your resume should fit on one page and should be tailored to the job you are looking for. Although you may have one standard resume that you give to companies, you will probably have different versions of your resume depending on the company and the job you are applying for.

When you customize your resume to the job and position, you increase your chances of getting an interview. Of course, it takes more time to write a separate resume for every position you are interested in, and it may not be feasible to do this if you are applying for a large number of jobs at one time. Whenever possible, however, you should try to tailor your resume to the position and company you are sending it to.

► How to Write a Resume

There are several formats that a resume can follow. Here are the basic categories of information that can be included in your resume—all of this information may not fit on one page, so you will have to decide which information is most important for your purpose.

> **THINK ABOUT IT**
>
> Writing a resume is not a one-time event. Your resume will change over time and for different purposes. It's a good idea to keep an ongoing record of your skills, jobs, and other credentials. Then, use your list to help you keep your resume up to date.

Heading. Your heading goes at the top of your resume. It includes your name, address (both your school and your permanent address if they are different), telephone number, and e-mail address. To save space, you can run some of this information, such as your address, phone number, and e-mail address across one line. It's often a good idea to have your name stand out: use a larger type size and boldfacing.

Summary. Some resumes include a summary, but in most cases this is not needed and takes up valuable space that could be better used in another category. If you have an unusual situation or credential that you want to explain—a summary is one place to do that. You can also use your cover letter for this information.

Objective. Many resumes include an objective that tells what kind of position you are looking for. Again, this information is usually included in your cover letter, so you can omit this category if you have other items you need to fit on one page.

Education. List any degrees or certificates you have received—with the most recent degree first. Include the name of the degree or certificate, the name of the institution you received it from, and the date you received it. You can also list your major and minor areas of study, your grade point average, special honors you received upon graduation, projects or research you completed as part of your degree, and other types of related and impressive information.

Experience/Work Experience. List past jobs, internships, and volunteer work you have done—with the most recent experience first. Include the name of your position, the name of the company, and the dates that you worked there. Below each job, summarize your responsibilities in the position. List your responsibilities in order of importance—either by their importance to your job or by their relevance to the new job you want.

Use action verbs to describe what you did. Include facts, dates, and try to quantify your experience as much as possible. Quantifying your experience is using numbers or statistics to tell how many, how often, how much, and so on. For example, rather than saying you increased the membership of a club, tell by how much—by 50 students, by 20%, and so on. Rather than saying you worked with several offices, tell how many offices you worked with.

collect	eliminate	institute
communicate	encourage	instruct
compare	engage	integrate
compile	enlarge	interpret
complete	enlist	interview
compose	establish	initiate
coordinate	estimate	introduce
conceive	evaluate	investigate
conduct	examine	involve
consolidate	expand	launch
contract	explain	lead
contribute	expedite	learn
control	facilitate	lecture
correct	follow up	locate
correspond	forecast	maintain
counsel	formulate	manage
create	foster	market
deal with	found	mediate
decrease	gather	modify
define	generate	monitor
delegate	guide	motivate
demonstrate	handle	negotiate
describe	help	observe
designate	identify	order
determine	illustrate	organize
develop	implement	originate
direct	improve	participate
document	increase	perceive
draft	influence	perform
edit	inform	pinpoint
educate	input	prepare
effect	inspect	present

process	reinforce	streamline
produce	remodel	study
program	reorganize	submit
promote	report	succeed
propose	research	suggest
prove	resolve	summarize
provide	revamp	supervise
publish	review	supply
purchase	revise	support
put together	schedule	survey
raise	screen	teach
receive	select	test
recommend	sell	train
reconcile	solve	translate
recruit	spoke	transcribe
reduce	start	tutor
reevaluate	stimulate	update
refer	structure	wrote

Use the past tense of these verbs for jobs you no longer do. It's okay to use the present tense for the things you do in your current job.

Extracurricular Activities/Other Experience. If you have other experience you want to highlight: you were treasurer of a club, a member of student government, or held a leadership or other position of responsibility in an association—you can list it here. As with your work experience, you should list your position or title, the name of the organization, and your dates of involvement. Under each entry, summarize your responsibilities in the position. You can list the experience in reverse chronological order as you do in the Work Experience section. Or, you can list it in order of importance or relevance to the position for which you are applying.

Achievements/Awards/Fellowships. Here you can list any specific achievements, awards, scholarships, fellowships, or grants that you want to highlight.

Special Skills/Other Skills. Under this heading, you might list fluency in a language other than English, particular computer skills, or other special training you might have on office equipment or in a computer programming language.

References. If you have space, list the full name, title, address, and telephone number of two to four people who have agreed to be a reference for you. Make sure the people you list have agreed in advance and are aware that you are using their names in your resume. If space on your resume is limited, it's acceptable to simply write "References available upon request." You can also provide references on a separate sheet of paper or on the company's application form.

PRACTICE ▶

Check your answers against the answer key at the back of the book.

1. Use one of the prewriting strategies in Section I to sketch out the information you might include in your resume. Make a list of the categories you think you might use and the information you might include under each category.

_____

_____

_____

_____

_____

_____

_____

_____

_____

_____

_____

_____

_____

_____

WRITING TIP

If you have experience or credentials that just don't fit into any of these headings, consider making up one of your own. Make sure the heading is clear and concise. Making up your own heading has the advantage of emphasizing a particular skill set or experience you have that matches the qualifications of the position you are seeking. Here are some examples of other headings you could use in your resume.

Accomplishments

Achievements

Career Profile

Career-Related Skills

Career Training

Community Service

Continuing Education

Computer Literacy

Honors and Awards

Internships

Language Proficiency

Leadership Skills

Licenses and Certification

Memberships

Military Experience

Presentations

Professional Development Seminars

Publications

Qualifications

Relevant Coursework

Summary of Skills

Supervisory Experience

Special Projects

Teaching Experience

Technical Training

Volunteer Work

Let's look at an example of a resume. (Additional examples can be found in the Appendix.)

Example

MELISSA R. RABIN
123 Cherry Blossom Drive
Palo Alto, CA 94304
(605) 555-7122, e-mail: mrabin@email.net

EDUCATION
CALIFORNIA COMMUNITY COLLEGE, Palo Alto, CA
Associate Degree, Business Administration, May 1999

EXPERIENCE
JOHNSON INSURANCE, Palo Alto, CA   1999–present
Administrative Assistant
- Maintained all files for an insurance agency
- Created and set up a new filing system used by three departments in the agency
- Trained five other staff members on word processing software

MACY'S, Palo Alto, CA   1997–1999
Sales Associate
- Sold clothing to customers and monitored inventory
- Exceeded monthly sales quotas by 12%

MCI, Palo Alto, CA   Summer 1996
- Verified customer accounts and answered questions

HOPE SOUP KITCHEN, Palo Alto, CA   Summer 1996
Project Manager
- Stocked the food pantry, prepared and served hot meals to families, and cleaned the kitchen and the dining hall two days per week

SPECIAL SKILLS AND AWARDS
- Fluent in Spanish
- Proficient in the use of Macintosh and IBM-compatible computers; familiar with MS Office
- Most Valuable Team Player Award, MCI (July 1996)

WRITING TIP

Keep these tips in mind when you write your resume:

Be concise. You don't even need complete sentences. Leave out pronouns, such as I, and start with your action verbs. Your writing style should be direct, clear, simple, and easy to follow. Get to the point!

Keep the format easy to follow, too. You don't want a cramped, crowded resume. Leave some white space and make the important information jump out at the reader.

Be polite and formal. Avoid slang, clichés, contractions, and informal language.

Use action verbs. Use the list in this lesson to help you describe your experience. When you can, avoid the passive voice and passive-like phrases, such as "served as" or "functioned as."

PRACTICE ▶

Check your answers against the answer key at the back of the book.

2. Think about a job or other position you have had. Then, write an entry you could include on your resume to tell a prospective employer about your experience in this position.

_____

_____

_____

_____

3. Create your own resume using the strategies in this lesson. Use the blank pages at the end of this book for your work.

▶ PUBLISHING YOUR RESUME

In the past, most resumes were typed on heavy weight stationery and mailed or hand-delivered. Today, you have more options for publishing your resume. Here are the pros and cons for each option.

FORM	PROS	CONS
Paper resume intended for traditional mail or hand delivery	You can use design and layout features to highlight your qualifications and make your resume stand out from the crowd. Paper resumes are easy to mail, fax, attach to an application, or hand out when you visit a company.	It's difficult for companies to scan resumes with design features. You can go overboard designing your resume and turn your potential employer off. Besides, it takes skill and time to produce such a resume.
Scannable resume—intended for a computer to scan into a database	A scannable resume has few design features and takes a short amount of time to put together on a computer. It also requires little design or word processing skill. These resumes can be submitted by mail, fax, or e-mail. They are easily scanned by a company's computer. The company can then search a large number of resumes for keywords in searching for a candidate. Many companies require a scannable resume. If yours isn't scannable, you may not be considered for the job.	It's more difficult to get your resume to stand out from others.
Electronic resume	Electronic resumes can be submitted to companies by e-mail, through the company's website, and via other recruiting websites. It's also very portable and easy to manipulate and update. Electronic resumes with little formatting are scannable.	You'll need to print your resume to hand it out or mail it to others.
Web-based resume (included in a website)	These resumes can be posted online and may attract more readers—although not necessarily a more targeted group of readers. You can add hyperlinks to your resume and fancy design features that are not available in other media.	Web-based resumes can be more difficult to print. You need to know how to design and author a website. You'll also need access to a Web hosting service.

▶ WHAT ARE COVER LETTERS?

Have you ever responded to a "want-ad" in the newspaper? If so, you probably sent the company a letter telling them about your interest in and qualifications for the job along with your resume. A cover letter is an introduction to your resume and a request to be interviewed for a job. It's an opportunity for you to highlight specific experiences or qualifications you have that aren't explained in your resume. Unlike a resume, a cover letter is subjective—it's your opinion of how your background prepares you for the job. Moreover, a cover letter is often the first encounter you have with a company, so you want to make good first impression.

▶ HOW TO WRITE A COVER LETTER

Like all forms of business writing, cover letters have a specific format and style. A standard cover letter usually has four paragraphs.

PARAGRAPH 1

The main purpose of the first paragraph is to convince the reader to keep reading. You should introduce yourself to the employer: explain your purpose in writing and name the job or position you want to be considered for. If you know of a specific job opening at the company, you should tell how you heard about the opening in the first paragraph—from a person, from an ad in the newspaper, from the company's website, from a career fair, and so on. This is also the place to mention any other ties you have to the company—for example, if someone you know works for the company and recommended that you apply for the job, you might mention the person's name in the first paragraph.

Examples: You might find these types of sentences in the first paragraph of a cover letter.
- This letter is to express my interest in . . .
- I am very interested in working for XYZ Company as a . . .
- I would like to be considered for XYZ Company's Credit Manager position . . .
- I recently read your announcement in the *Times* for a . . .
- I recently received some information about an opportunity to work at XYZ Company . . .
- Lee MacDonald, a former associate of yours, recommended that I contact you about . . .

> **WRITING TIP**
>
> It's important to personalize each cover letter. Here are some ways to personalize each letter.
>
> ▸ **Address the letter to a person.** Try to find the name and title of someone who works at the company. You might have to call the company and ask for the name of someone in Human Resources, in

Personnel, or in the department you want to work in. If you absolutely cannot find a person to address your letter to, then it's acceptable to address your letter to Sir/Madam—but it's not nearly as effective as addressing a specific person.

▸ **Use a different cover letter for each job inquiry.** Although there are some cases in which a mass mailing of a form letter works, in general, you should write each cover letter with a specific company and job in mind. You can often recycle parts of a standard cover letter or an inventory of your skills. However, every company and every job are different—and your cover letter should reflect that.

PARAGRAPH 2

In the second paragraph, you should show how you are a good match for the company. Often, this will require doing some research on the company beforehand.

Examples: You might find these types of sentences in the second paragraph of a cover letter.

- I am a good match for XYZ Company because . . .
- Based on my research, I am convinced that my values are a good match with those of XYZ Company. For example, . . .
- I have the skills to do a good job at XYZ Company. For example, . . .
- I am particularly well-suited to working at XYZ Company because . . .

WRITING TIP

Keep your reader's point of view in mind as you write. Your writing should focus on the *employer's needs*. Rather than telling all the things you hope to learn from the company or the things you hope to get from the company, stick with what *you can do for the company*.

PARAGRAPH 3

Here, you should give specific details about yourself and show how they relate to the job you are applying for. You want to show that you are qualified to do the job well.

Examples: You might find these types of sentences in the third paragraph of a cover letter.

- My major is in business, and I have taken a number of courses in computer programming . . .
- I have taken a number of classes in statistics, and I used statistics in my senior project . . .
- I have served as a language exchange partner in conjunction with the Intensive Language Institute . . .
- I recruited volunteers for and managed a project at XYZ Charities . . .
- As you can see from my resume, . . .

WRITING TIP

Support your claims with specific examples.

Instead of saying this:	Back it up with examples like this:
I am a quick learner.	I am a quick learner. This past summer, I was commended by my supervisors at XYZ Company for my ability to learn about the organization and contribute to projects in a relatively short amount of time.
I am a leader at school.	I am a leader at school. As President of the University Math Club, I implemented several new programs, such as peer tutoring and a math competition—and increased membership by 30%.
I am a good team player.	I am a good team player. In fact, my supervisors at XYZ Company said that my teamwork skills are one of my strongest qualities and

	stated that I did an *outstanding job* collaborating with coworkers on my last project.
No matter what a job demands, I am willing to work hard to succeed in that position.	No matter what a job demands, I am willing to work hard to succeed in that position. Unlike most of my peers in the car insurance business, I entered the field with little knowledge of cars and claims adjusting. And yet, I advanced rapidly. I consistently completed training courses at the top of the class. I also sought out mentors within the organization and spent extra time before and after work asking questions and practicing my adjusting skills. I completed additional courses in my spare time.
I have a lot of experience helping my peers.	I have a lot of experience helping my peers. I was a student adviser for three semesters and a mentor for transfer students for two semesters. I also tutored other students at the Learning Skills Center.

PARAGRAPH 4

The last paragraph is your conclusion. As with all writing, you want to conclude with a take-home message. Your take-home message will usually be that you are qualified for the job and would like to interview for the position. It's also a good idea to set a goal for the next step. For example, you might indicate that you will call the person in one week.

Examples: You might find these types of sentences in the last paragraph of a cover letter.

- I will be in your area next week. I will call on Monday to request an interview . . .
- I want to reiterate my interest in working for XYZ Company . . .
- I am confident that I have the skills to . . .
- I think you will find that my qualifications match those you are looking for . . .
- If I do not hear from you next week, I will call . . .
- If you need any more information, please contact me at . . .
- I look forward to meeting with you soon . . .

THINK ABOUT IT

Do what you say you are going to do. If you say in the last paragraph that you will call next week, you should call next week. If you say that you are available in the evenings after 6 P.M., then you should try to be home and available to talk at this time.

Let's look at an example of a cover letter.

Example

Paragraph 1: The writer tells his purpose in writing and names the position he is interested in. He also tells how he heard about the position.

Paragraph 2: The writer aligns himself with two characteristics he has found are important to XYZ Company through his research: customer service and knowledge of technology.

September 26, 2001
1234 Modella Drive
Little Rock, AR 45890

Ms. Joan Hamood
Campus Recruiter
XYZ Company
College Town, NY 10002

Dear Ms. Hamood:

I enjoyed speaking with you Friday at the Home Town Community College Career Fair. As I mentioned then, I would like to be considered for XYZ Company's internship this summer. I have two years of work experience, and I am currently pursuing an associate degree in Technology at Home Town Community College. My resume is attached.

Based on my research, I am convinced that I am a good match with XYZ Company. I am passionate about technology, and I enjoy dealing with people and customers. As a customer service representative at Jones Repair Services—a company with thirty employees— I was awarded Employee of the Month twice in one year. In addition, I have maintained a B or better in all my technology courses at Home Town Community College. My ability to serve customers and my knowledge of technology are a good match for XYZ Company's needs.

I also have the strong time-management and teamwork skills that you mentioned would be key to this position. During the last year, I have worked part-time while going to College Town Community College. Juggling both work and college has helped me refine my time-management skills and learn more efficient ways of getting things done. My grade point average has stayed above a 3.0, and I haven't been late to work once during this time. A good example of my teamwork skills is the role I played in the Community College's blood drive. Last spring I worked with a team of four other students to set a blood drive goal, advertise the event, and recruit student volunteers. We exceeded our goal of pints donated by 10%.

Please review my attached resume. I think you will find that I am qualified to do a good job for XYZ Company this summer. In addition, I have the drive to work very hard. Please contact me at 432-555-7890, if you need more information. I look forward to talking with you about the internship. I will give you a call next week to set up a time to meet.

Sincerely,

Thomas Perez, Jr.

Thomas Perez, Jr.
Enclosure: Resume

Paragraph 4: He ends with a strong take-home message and sets a goal for the next step in the process.

Paragraph 3: The writer gives examples of his time-management and teamwork skills—two skills he learned are important to the position he is seeking.

WRITING TIP

Keep these tips in mind when you write a cover letter.

Be concise. Cover letters are not an opportunity to dazzle your audience with fancy or flowery language. Your writing style should be clear, simple, and easy to follow. Get to the point!

Be polite and formal. Avoid slang, clichés, contractions, and informal language.

Use action verbs. Action verbs are those that clearly show you as a valuable employee.

PRACTICE ▶

Check your answers against the answer key at the back of the book.

4. Assume that you want to apply for a job that requires the following qualifications. Write a sentence giving a personal example of each qualification.

a. Oral and written communication skills

_____

_____

b. Leadership skills

_____

_____

_____

c. Teamwork skills

_____

_____

d. Problem-solving skills

_____

_____

5. Write a cover letter. Use the blank pages at the back of this book for your work.

▶ FORMATTING TIPS

- Always type your cover letter and resume.
- Use a standard business letter format for the cover letter. The next lesson walks you through business letter basics, if you're not sure what standard business letter format is.
- Use the same font and paper for your cover letter and your resume. 12 point Times New Roman is a good choice of font. Heavy-weight white or ivory paper is a good choice of paper.
- Check your letter and resume for spelling, grammar, punctuation, and usage. Be especially careful to spell the person's name and the name of the company correctly in your cover letter. It's also a good idea to have several other people read your documents for spelling, grammar, punctuation, and usage, too, before sending them out. Resumes with these types of errors often find themselves in the trash can.

17 ▶ Writing Business Letters

LESSON SUMMARY

You probably get them in the mail all the time, and they all look pretty similar. They are business letters. This lesson shows you the basic parts of a business letter. You'll also learn the different ways of formatting a business letter.

Your boss asks you to write a letter to a disgruntled customer. Your department receives the wrong shipment or is billed the wrong amount for office supplies. You need to explain your company's procedures to a new client. These things can and do happen, and you may be the one responsible for writing the business letter that helps resolve the situation.

▶ WRITING BUSINESS LETTERS

Business letters are usually sent to people outside your company. They are also sometimes used within a company for more formal situations, to convey important information, or to communicate between departments or divisions of the same company. Let's discuss the main parts of a business letter. Then, we'll look at some examples.

DATE

Business letters should be dated with the date the letter is completed and sent. Sometimes, it can take several days to complete a business letter (you may have multiple drafts or need to wait for a supervisor's approval before you can send a letter)—use the last day you worked on the letter in these cases. Write out the month, day, and year: October 12, 2001. Don't abbreviate the month or include the day of the week.

SENDER'S ADDRESS

Most companies and many individuals have their own letterhead. When letterhead stationery is available and appropriate for your use, you should use it for business letters. If your company doesn't have letterhead stationery or if you are writing a business letter as an individual to a company and you do not have a personal letterhead, then you will need to type your full address before the date.

READER'S ADDRESS

The reader's address is also called the inside address—it includes the name of the person and the place you are sending your letter. Write out the full name of the person, his or her title, the company, and the address of the company. Avoid abbreviations—only Mr., Mrs., Ms., Dr., and the state should be abbreviated.

WRITING TIP

The following state abbreviations are recognized by the U. S. Postal Service. You can use them in your business letters and on the envelopes.

Alabama	AL	Missouri	MO
Alaska	AK	Montana	MT
Arizona	AZ	Nebraska	NE
Arkansas	AR	Nevada	NV
California	CA	New Hampshire	NH
Colorado	CO	New Jersey	NJ
Connecticut	CT	New Mexico	NM
Delaware	DE	New York	NY
District of Columbia	DC	North Carolina	NC
Florida	FL	North Dakota	ND
Georgia	GA	Ohio	OH
Hawaii	HI	Oklahoma	OK
Idaho	ID	Oregon	OR
Illinois	IL	Pennsylvania	PA
Indiana	IN	Rhode Island	RI
Iowa	IA	South Carolina	SC
Kansas	KS	South Dakota	SD
Kentucky	KT	Tennessee	TN
Louisiana	LA	Texas	TX
Maine	ME	Utah	UT
Maryland	MD	Vermont	VT
Massachusetts	MA	Washington	WA
Michigan	MI	West Virginia	WV
Minnesota	MN	Wisconsin	WI
Mississippi	MS	Wyoming	WY

SUBJECT LINE

This is a brief phrase telling the main idea of the letter. It is optional—many business letters do not include this line. It usually comes before the salutation, but it can also come after the salutation. Often the subject is preceded by *re:* (an abbreviation for *regarding*) and is sometimes underlined or boldfaced for emphasis. If you use a subject line, make sure it tells your reader quickly and effectively what the letter is about. The following are some examples.

Examples

Subject: Billing Error

Re: Account #3290

Re: New Security Measures

SALUTATION

The salutation is your greeting. Salutations begin with the word *Dear* and are always followed by a colon— not a comma. Here are some examples:

IF YOU	THEN WRITE	EXAMPLES
Know the recipient and typically address him or her by first name	The recipient's first name	Dear Jo Ann: Dear Sameer:
Are not on a first-name basis with the recipient	Mr./Mrs./Ms./Dr. + the recipient's last name	Dear Mr. Jones: Dear Mrs. Ishak: Dear Ms. Patel: Dear Dr. Swenson:
Know the recipient's name, but don't know the recipient's gender	Mr./Ms. + the recipient's last name, the recipient's full name, or a generic salutation, such as To Whom It May Concern or Sir/Madam	Dear Mr./Ms. Harrings: Dear Chris Harrings: Dear E. C. James: To Whom It May Concern: Sir/Madam:
Don't know the reader's name	A generic salutation, such as To Whom It May Concern or Sir/Madam or the person's title	To Whom It May Concern: Sir/Madam: Dear Customer Service Representative: Dear Marketing Analyst:

BODY

The body of the business letter is your message. It usually consists of three or more paragraphs. The first paragraph should begin in a friendly, concise way telling the main idea of the business letter. The middle paragraphs should deliver the point of the business letter. Each paragraph should have a topic sentence and supporting details, just as any other good paragraph should. It's appropriate, especially in longer business letters, to use headings and/or bulleted lists in order to make it easier for your reader to digest the information. The body ends with a concluding paragraph. Your concluding paragraph should restate the purpose of the letter and give a take-home message. Often, the take-home message will request specific information or a specific action on the part of the reader. Each body paragraph is usually typed single space. Double space in between the paragraphs.

Use these questions to guide your writing of the body of a business letter.

- What are the main points I need to make in this letter?
- How should I sequence my points?
- How can I use headings and lists to better organize this information?
- How can I use boldfacing to emphasize parts of this information?
- Is there information I can leave out of this letter? What information does the reader really not need to know?
- What is my take-home message?

CLOSING

End your letter with a polite good-bye. Here are some ways to close:

Sincerely,	Best regards,
Sincerely yours,	Yours truly,
Respectfully,	Regards,
Cordially,	Thank you,

Notice that only the first word is capitalized. The closing is followed by a comma.

SIGNATURE

Follow your closing with four blank lines. Then, type your full name. Beneath your typed name, type your full title. If you plan to mail, fax, or hand-deliver a hard copy of your letter, you should sign your name in the space between your closing and your typed full name. Sometimes, letters are sent electronically—in this case, it is not necessary to sign your name.

TYPIST'S REFERENCE

In the past, this line has been used to indicate that someone other than the sender of the letter typed the letter. For example, if your name is Donna Richardson and your secretary's name is Maria Sanchez, you might use this reference at the end of your letter: DR/ms. Notice that the writer's initials are capitalized and the typist's initials are in lower case letters. This indicates that you wrote the letter, but your secretary typed it. With the widespread use of computers and computer literacy these days, many people type their own letters. In this case, you don't need to include your initials as the writer or the typist. However, you might use this line to indicate how the document has been saved, filed, or stored on the computer.

ENCLOSURES

Often, you will need to include other documents with a business letter. When you do, you should include a line to indicate that other documents are enclosed. It's a good idea to list the documents you are enclosing so that you make your reader aware of what is supposed to be included in the letter. Here's an example:

Enclosures: Outline of proposed changes
                     Schedule of changes
                     Budget for making the changes

It's also acceptable to abbreviate: *Enc.* Here's an example:

Enc.:   Appendix B

CC:/DISTRIBUTION

If you will be sending your letter to people other than the named recipient at the top of the letter, you can list these other people here after the letters cc: or CC:. These letters stand for carbon copy. List the names of the other recipients either in alphabetical order or by rank. You can include each person's title, if you would like. Generally, if the information in the letter involves or references other people, you should consider sending a copy of the letter to them as well.

▶ FORMATTING BUSINESS LETTERS

There are three main ways to format a business letter: block format, modified semi-block format, and semi-block format. Here is how they compare.

BLOCK FORMAT	MODIFIED BLOCK FORMAT	SEMI-BLOCK FORMAT
Each part of the letter is left-justified, or set up against the left margin. This is probably the most common and simplest format for business letters.	The recipient's name, company, address, salutation, and the body of the letter are all left-justified. The date, closing, and signature are each aligned down the middle of the page.	The recipient's name, company, address, and salutation are all left-justified. Each paragraph of the body of the letter is left-justified and indented. The date, closing, and signature are each aligned down the middle of the page. This is probably the least common format used for business letters.

WRITING TIP

Many companies have their own guidelines for writing business letters. If your company has its own way of doing things—even if it contradicts this book—you should follow your company's guidelines.

Let's look at some examples of business letters and formats.

Example: Block Format

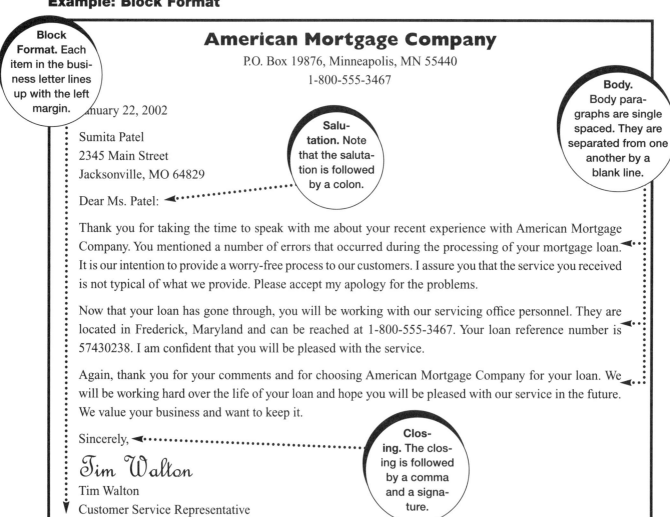

Block Format. Each item in the business letter lines up with the left margin.

American Mortgage Company

P.O. Box 19876, Minneapolis, MN 55440

1-800-555-3467

January 22, 2002

Sumita Patel
2345 Main Street
Jacksonville, MO 64829

Dear Ms. Patel:

Salutation. Note that the salutation is followed by a colon.

Thank you for taking the time to speak with me about your recent experience with American Mortgage Company. You mentioned a number of errors that occurred during the processing of your mortgage loan. It is our intention to provide a worry-free process to our customers. I assure you that the service you received is not typical of what we provide. Please accept my apology for the problems.

Now that your loan has gone through, you will be working with our servicing office personnel. They are located in Frederick, Maryland and can be reached at 1-800-555-3467. Your loan reference number is 57430238. I am confident that you will be pleased with the service.

Again, thank you for your comments and for choosing American Mortgage Company for your loan. We will be working hard over the life of your loan and hope you will be pleased with our service in the future. We value your business and want to keep it.

Sincerely,

Tim Walton

Tim Walton
Customer Service Representative

Body. Body paragraphs are single spaced. They are separated from one another by a blank line.

Closing. The closing is followed by a comma and a signature.

Example: Modified Block Format

Mod-ified Block Format. The date, closing, and signature align in the center of the page.

FANCY CHIPS

1003 FRANKFORD AVENUE / JACKSONVILLE, TX 75766

PHONE: 548-555-8904 / FAX: 548-555-7004

WEBSITE: WWW.FANCYCHIPS.COM

March 29, 2002

Jean-Luc Bibaud
24 Main Street
New Summerville, MA 02821

Dear Mr. Bibaud:

Thank you for your recent letter about the black substance you found in a package of Fancy Potato Chips. We have analyzed the substance you provided and determined that it is simply a piece of charred potato. I apologize for any inconvenience this may have caused you.

We take a lot of pride in the quality of our chips and make every effort to keep charred pieces of potatoes from being packaged with our Fancy Chips products. In fact, we filter the oil used to fry the potatoes and clean our equipment regularly. We also carry out visual inspections of our chips before they are packaged. Although we take these measures, sometimes a piece of burned potato will make its way into a package of our Fancy Potato Chips.

Please accept my apology for the unpleasant experience you had with Fancy Potato Chips. I am enclosing coupons for two free packages of Fancy Potato Chips and hope that you will find these packages exceed your expectations. Please do not hesitate to contact me again if you have any other problems or concerns about our products.

Regards,

LaToya Jones

LaToya Jones
Customer Service Representative

The other items in the business letter are left-justified.

Example: Semi-Block Format

Publish Yourself! Inc.

P.O. Box 783 • Jasper, ND 34902

Phone: 819-555-8923 • Fax: 819-555-7834

Website: www.publishyourselfnow!com

April 9, 2001

Meinrad Meister

2894 Snow White Drive

Mansfield, FL 69821

Dear Mr. Meister:

I am an editor at Publish Yourself! In reviewing your recent manuscript, I have found three figures that are a part of another publication by your colleague Dr. Johnson.

We cannot reprint figures that have been previously published elsewhere without a letter of permission from the copyright holder. Although I recognize that Dr. Johnson is an acquaintance of yours, we still need a letter of permission before we can proceed. Generally, the copyright is held by the publisher of the publication rather than the author. If Dr. Johnson does indeed hold the copyright, then we simply need a letter from the publisher stating this along with a letter from Dr. Johnson giving us permission to use his figures in your book.

I am sending you a sample letter that you can use to request permission to use these figures. Usually if a request is written on the author's letterhead, the publisher responds more quickly. So you might request that Dr. Johnson assist you in this task. I am also attaching a copy of our copyright policy.

I look forward to receiving your letters of permission so that we can continue work on your book. If you have any questions, please contact me directly at 819-555-1111.

Yours truly,

Manny Jimenez

Manny Jimenez

Permissions Editor

Enclosures: Request for Permission to Reprint Form

Publish Yourself! Copyright Policy

Check your answers against the answer key at the back of the book.

1. Read two business letters. They can be letters that you received or letters that you have written yourself. Then, answer the following questions about each letter.

Letter 1
a. What is the main idea of the letter?

_____

_____

_____

b. How is the letter formatted? Does it follow one of the formats shown in this lesson? If so, which one?

_____

_____

c. What is your overall impression of the letter? Is it polite? Is it effective? Explain your answer.

_____

_____

_____

_____

_____

Letter 2
d. What is the main idea of the letter?

_____

_____

_____

e. How is the letter formatted? Does it follow one of the formats shown in this lesson? If so, which one?

_____

_____

f. What is your overall impression of the letter? Is it polite? Is it effective? Explain your answer.

_____

_____

_____

_____

_____

2. Write a business letter using one of the formats described in this lesson. If you need more space than is provided below, use the blank pages at the end of this book for your work.

_____

_____

_____

_____

_____

_____

_____

_____

_____

_____

_____

_____

_____

_____

_____

_____

_____

_____

_____

_____

_____

_____

_____

_____

_____

_____

_____

_____

_____

_____

_____

_____

_____

_____

_____

Writing Memos and E-mails

LESSON SUMMARY

If you have a job, you know that a lot of time can be spent reading and writing memos and e-mails at work. In this lesson, you'll learn the basics of how to write these forms of correspondence effectively.

emos and e-mails are used for different communication situations at work, and each has a specific format and rules. In this lesson, we'll take a look at each one.

▶ WRITING MEMOS

What's the difference between a memo and a business letter? Here are some common differences:

MEMOS USUALLY (BUT NOT ALWAYS)	LETTERS USUALLY (BUT NOT ALWAYS)
Are written to people inside your company	Are written to people who work outside your company or in another department
Are initialed by the sender	Are signed by the sender
Vary in length from a couple of sentences to many pages long	Are less than two or three pages long
Are informal	Are formal

Memos generally have six parts.

- **To**—tells who the memo is addressed to. You might address a memo to one person or to an entire distribution list. When you are addressing a specific person in a memo, use the person's full name and title.
- **From**—gives your name or the names of the authors of the memo. This line could include several people or be your department's name.
- **Date**—tells the date that the memo was written. Use the most recent date if the memo was written over a period of time.
- **Subject or *Re***—tells the topic of the memo. Try to be specific.
- **cc**—as in business letters, sometimes this is used to list the names of people who should receive the memo, but are not named as recipients of the memo.
- **Body**—reports the message of the memo.

Memos can be printed on plain white paper, on a specific memo form, or on official letterhead. Some memos are even handwritten on a memo pad. Here are three common memo formats.

Examples

```
To:
From:
Date:
Subject:
```

```
Date:
Subject:
To:
From:
```

<table>
<tr><td>Subject:</td><td>Date:</td></tr>
<tr><td>To:</td><td>From:</td></tr>
</table>

Now let's look at some examples of memos.

Example

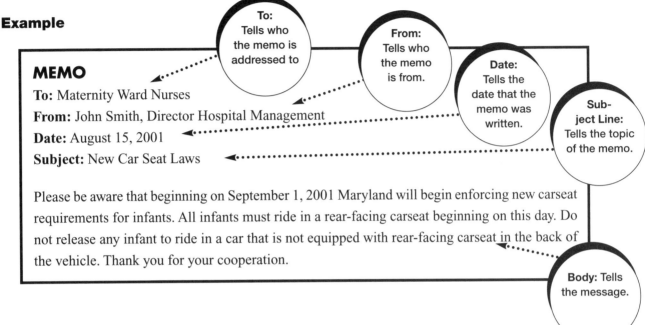

MEMO

To: Maternity Ward Nurses
From: John Smith, Director Hospital Management
Date: August 15, 2001
Subject: New Car Seat Laws

Please be aware that beginning on September 1, 2001 Maryland will begin enforcing new carseat requirements for infants. All infants must ride in a rear-facing carseat beginning on this day. Do not release any infant to ride in a car that is not equipped with rear-facing carseat in the back of the vehicle. Thank you for your cooperation.

To: Tells who the memo is addressed to

From: Tells who the memo is from.

Date: Tells the date that the memo was written.

Subject Line: Tells the topic of the memo.

Body: Tells the message.

Example

MEMORANDUM

Date: July 19, 2002

Subject: Break Room Closed Next Week

To: All Employees

From: Human Resources Department

The Employee Break Room will be closed all next week—July 22 through July 26. We will be remodeling the break room during this time. The break room will reopen on July 29.

We apologize for any inconvenience this may cause you. We are putting patio tables and chairs on the back patio for your use while the break room is closed. We're looking forward to unveiling the remodeled break room on July 29 with an ice cream social. Details about that coming soon!

There is more than one approach to writing memos. A common approach is to dive right in—giving your most important information first. Then, you follow up with the details. Many people believe it is the most effective approach, too. Here's an example of this approach—notice the most important information is in the first sentence of the memo.

Example

We need volunteers to help clean up the highway in front of our building. As you know, Lois & Kolby Marketing is responsible for cleaning up litter along the two mile segment of highway in front of our building. We have committed to one highway clean up per quarter of this year. Our next highway clean up is March 12—next Saturday. Can we count on you? Breakfast, lunch, gloves, and garbage bags will be provided.

Another approach is to lead up to the most important information—it's almost the last sentence in this version of the memo—and to grab the reader's attention first. Here's an example.

Example

Can we count on you to help save the environment and beautify the grounds outside our building? As you know, Lois & Kolby Marketing is responsible for cleaning up litter along the two-mile segment of highway in front of our building. We have committed to one highway clean up per quarter of this year. Our next highway clean up is March 12—next

> Saturday. We need volunteers to help clean up the highway in front of our building. Breakfast, lunch, gloves, and garbage bags will be provided.

PRACTICE ▶

Check your answers against the answer key at the back of the book.

1. Write a memo using one of the formats described in this lesson.

_____
_____
_____
_____
_____
_____
_____
_____
_____
_____
_____
_____
_____
_____
_____
_____
_____
_____

▶ WRITING E-MAIL MESSAGES

Like memos, e-mail messages begin with a header that includes a *to, from, date,* and *subject* line. In many ways, e-mail messages are electronic memos. Keep the following tips in mind when you write e-mail messages at work.

- **Keep your message short and to the point.** E-mail is not the medium for a 10-page essay, unless you are sending it as an attachment to your e-mail message for the reader to print out and read at another time. It's harder to read on screen than on paper. Moreover, people do not have a lot of time to read e-mail, and they receive far more than they'd like to every day.

- **Write your e-mail messages carefully.** Even though you can write and send an e-mail message in a just a few minutes, you should always read over and revise what you have written before pushing the send button. Quickly sent e-mails are often regretted because they are poorly worded, unclear, or were sent in a moment of anger.

- **Keep the format simple.** When possible, use headings, lists, and other ways of breaking up the text. You can use capital letters for emphasis, but don't type an entire message in all caps—it's hard to read, and it's commonly considered virtual shouting. Other formatting, such as italics, bullets, tables, and graphs, can be lost in an e-mail message.

- **Use an appropriate tone and level of formality.** When you're writing, it's easy to forget about the person who will be reading your e-mail message. If you are in an e-mail conversation, try to keep the tone (and length) of your reply in line with the rest of the conversation. Don't assume a level of informality with a person you would otherwise communicate more formally with.

- **Take the time to check your e-mail for spelling, grammar, punctuation, and usage errors.** These types of errors reflect poorly on you and can cause confusion.

- **End with a signature.** An e-mail signature is text containing your contact information that comes at the end of your e-mail message. Many e-mail systems will automatically add your signature at the end of all your messages. Include this information in your work signature: your name, title, company, address, phone number, fax number, and company e-mail address.

WRITING TIP

As with other forms of writing, one of your main jobs in writing e-mails should be to make your reader's job as easy as you can. Think about your own e-mail inbox and how you feel when you go through the messages you receive. If you're like most people, you use the subject line to help you decide whether you'll even open an e-mail message. The subject line should tell your reader what your message is about. Here are some tips to make your subject lines effective.

- Don't send a message with an empty subject line.
- Write a meaningful subject line—one that describes the content of your message.
- When replying back and forth, it's helpful to change the subject line or start a new e-mail message with a new subject line when you change the topic.

Check your answers against the answer key at the back of the book.

2. Read the e-mail message below. Then evaluate the e-mail message using the information presented so far in this lesson. Use these questions to guide you.

Date: Mon, 1 Oct 2001 12:33:24 –0500
From: Sara Chang <schang@xyzcompany.com>
To: All Employees <group@xyzcompany.com>

Subject: Attention

SATURDAY, we will be getting new carpet in our office. To help with the carpet installation, you are asked to do the following things by FRIDAY at 5 PM. REMOVE all your belongings and non-furniture items from the carpet in your work area. REMOVE everything from the surfaces of the furniture in your work area. If you have any questions or need help complying with these requests, please call me at extension 555. Thanks for your cooperation!
Sara

a. Is the message short and to the point? Explain.

_____

_____

b. Does the message appear to have been carefully written? Explain.

_____

_____

c. Is the format simple and effective? Explain.

_____

_____

d. Does the e-mail message have any spelling, grammar, punctuation, or usage errors?

_____

_____

3. Correct any problems with the e-mail message you evaluated in question **1** above. Use the space below to rewrite the e-mail message.

_____
_____
_____
_____
_____
_____
_____
_____
_____
_____
_____
_____
_____
_____
_____

4. Choose an e-mail message that you have received or sent recently. Then evaluate the e-mail message using the information presented so far in this lesson. Use these questions to guide you.

a. Is the message short and to the point? Explain.

_____
_____
_____

b. Does the message appear to have been carefully written? Explain.

_____
_____
_____

c. Is the format simple and effective? Explain.

_____
_____
_____

d. Does the e-mail message have any spelling, grammar, punctuation, or usage errors?

_____
_____
_____

▶ How to Reply to an E-mail Message

A large part of sending e-mail messages is actually replying to messages you've received. Here are some tips to effectively replying to e-mail messages at work.

- **Provide a context for your reply.** Your reader may not instantly remember what has already been said. So include enough of the original message to give your reader a context for your reply.
- **Distinguish your reply from the original message.** For example, you can put the existing text in carats, like these "< . . . >". Another effective way to visually distinguish your reply from the original message is to set it in a different color of type.
- **Don't overquote past messages.** Over time, quoting past e-mail messages in replies can create a very long document and a great burden for your reader to sort through. Quote only the parts of an original message that you need for the context of your reply. When the conversation changes in topic, start a new thread rather than continuing to reply using an existing message.
- **Pay attention to where your reply will go.** Sometimes, replying to a message that has been sent to a list of people will actually send the message to ALL the people on the list. If you intend to reply to the entire distribution list, that's fine. But it can be quite embarrassing and irritating to the receivers if you really needed to respond to only one person on the list.
- **Write when you are calm.** Because e-mail messages can be sent very quickly, it's possible to get caught up in the heat of the moment and write an emotional—and perhaps inflammatory—reply to an e-mail. Always read your message before pushing send. If you are upset about an e-mail message you have received, it's okay to write a quick response right away—but don't send it yet. Save it to your draft folder, then move on to another task. Go back to your reply later when you are feeling more calm, and decide if you want to send the message. Just writing the message may diffuse your emotions and you might change your mind about your response.

▶ When to Send an E-mail Message

E-mail messages are very similar to memos. So how do you know when to e-mail and when to circulate a paper memo? Here are some questions to help you make this decision.

- **Does your message involve legal, official, or other information that you need to document in a paper file?** If so, you might want to use a paper memo. However, more and more companies are trying to become "paperless"—that is, to use less paper, so an e-mail message might still be okay for some information. Stick with a paper memo for legal matters, though.
- **Do you need a response to your message right away, but can't reach the person by phone?** An e-mail message is a good option in this case—especially if you know that the person checks his or her e-mail regularly.
- **Is the recipient a person who is hard to reach by phone and who checks his or her e-mail regularly?** An e-mail message is probably a good option, then. Another option is voicemail.

- Do you want the recipient to respond to your message at his or her leisure? E-mail is a good way to send your message in this case because the person can read and respond to your message whenever it's convenient.
- Is your message long or complicated? Will the recipient probably need to print it out to read it carefully? If so, a paper memo is probably a better bet than an e-mail message. E-mail messages are better suited for short, simple communication.

THINK ABOUT IT

Think twice before you send confidential, private, or other sensitive material in an e-mail message. E-mail messages can be intercepted. The information may reach people other than those you intend. Unless you are confident that the server is secure, you may not want to include information about yourself (Social Security number, credit card number, and so on) or your company's secrets (strategic plans for the future, account numbers, and so on). In fact, your company may have regulations about what can and cannot be sent over e-mail or the Internet. Find out and follow your company's guidelines.

Writing Reports

LESSON SUMMARY

As you move up at work, you'll probably be asked to write reports. In this lesson, you'll learn the basic parts of a report and some tips for writing effective reports.

t work, reports are used to give the progress of a project, to talk about an employee's performance over the last year, to propose making a change in a procedure or launching a new product. You'll probably encounter these kinds of reports at work:

- Meeting minutes—summarize what was discussed at a meeting
- Status reports—tell the current progress made on a certain project
- Travel reports—describe the different aspects of a business trip
- Expense reports—list the expenses incurred on a business trip
- Accident reports—describe an incident
- Performance appraisals—evaluate an employee's performance over a period of time
- Competitive analysis—compares your company's product with similar products put out by competitors

As you can see, reports are used a lot at work. When the same kind of report is used frequently in a work situation, there is often a standard format or maybe even an electronic template that you can use to write up the report. If your company doesn't give you a specific format or template to follow, you can use the guidelines in this lesson to write your reports.

▶ THE PARTS OF A REPORT

Reports generally have four main parts:

Introduction—introduces the topic and purpose of the report and may summarize the material in the report. You might find the following kinds of documents as parts of a report's introduction.

- A cover letter or memo explaining to whom the report is directed, why the report was written, how the data were gathered, the assumptions or limitations of the information included in the report, and so on
- A table of contents listing the main parts of the report
- A summary or abstract of the report telling the main idea and conclusions of the report (many readers will only read this part of the report!)

Body—gives your main idea and supporting details.

Recommendations—tells what action should be taken based on the information you have presented. Some short reports and form reports do not have explicit recommendations.

Supplementary material—backs up the information you've provided with data. Not all reports include supplementary materials. You might find these kinds of documents attached at the end of a report.

- Appendices including tables, graphs, raw data, sample forms, financial statements, and other materials that you do not expect your reader to read, but provide in case your reader wants to look up something specific
- Exhibits including charts, graphs, figures, and so on
- List of illustrations included in the report
- Glossary of technical terms or jargon used in the report
- Receipts, budgets, or other documents required for accounting or financial review

Let's look at a few examples of different kinds of reports. Not all reports are as short or as a simple as these examples are. However, they do all basically follow a similar format and have the same main parts.

Example: Status Report

Weekly Status Report

To: Eileen Jakobsen, Director of Marketing
Submitted by: Jill Hancock, Project Manager
Date: October 12, 2001

Schedule: We do not anticipate any problems completing the project on schedule as long as materials continue to come in as planned.

Budget: Finances are on target, for the moment. We have spent 45% of our budget for the project and are about 38% done with the project.

Tasks completed since last report:
Our team sent out questionnaires to 1000 customers asking them about their satisfaction level with the product.
We set up 10 of the 20 customer interviews planned for next month.
We outlined the product samples needed for the customer interviews.

Tasks planned for next week:
Arrange the remaining 10 interviews with customers planned for next month
Start getting together the interview questions we will use
Order the product samples needed for the interviews
Make the travel arrangements for Cindy and Georgia to go to the interview sites

Problems/Comments:
None at this time.

> **Introduction:** Notice that the introduction can be very simple. This introduction is basically a heading.

> **Body:** The body of this report is broken up with headings that help the reader find specific information. This is typical of reports and very effective.

Example: Employee Performance Appraisal

XYZ Company
Performance Appraisal

Employee Name: Sharmila Chowdhury
Employee Social Security No.: 333-33-3333
Employee Title: Summer Intern
Supervisor's Name and Title: Elaine Wallace, Director of Customer Support
Period covered: May 15, 2001 through August 15, 2001

I.   Summary of performance
Sharmila was very efficient this summer in gathering and compiling data from our other offices. The data she compiled is valuable for our Global Customer Support Project and will be used to better meet our customers' needs in the near future. Sharmila communicated professionally and

> **Introduction:** Notice that the introduction can be very simple. This introduction is basically a heading.

followed up promptly with all regional and local contacts. She worked tirelessly to get all the information needed. Using the data she had collected, Sharmila was able to begin a preliminary draft of recommendations for the future.

II. Characteristics of Effective Performance

Please check the rating and provide comments/examples where relevant.

[ ] **Exceeds Expectations (EE)**—check this rating when the employee has consistently exceeded your expectations in the area being rated.

[X] **Meets Expectations (ME)**—check this rating when the employee has achieved your expectations in most areas.

[ ] **Does Not Meet Expectations (DNME)**—check this rating when the employee's job performance in the area being rated is unacceptably low.

Leadership skills Sharmila demonstrated leadership in her ability to put together a contact list and effectively used it to gather the information needed for her project.	ME
Communication skills Sharmila communicated effectively with other offices as she acquired all the data needed in such a short amount of time.	ME
Initiative Sharmila showed initiative when she began an analysis and a preliminary draft of recommendations for the future using the data she had collected.	ME
Teamwork skills Sharmila did a very good job of working with our other offices and administrative staff this summer. Her ability to get along with others and to convince others to work showed true team spirit.	EE
Time-management skills Sharmila was able to manage her time well. She accomplished more on this project over the summer than our office had been able to accomplish in the six months preceding her internship. She met all the deadlines.	EE

Body: The body of this report is also divided by categories.

Recommendations for the future: Sharmila's performance this summer shows promise. If she is interested in becoming a permanent employee at XYZ Company, I recommend that she complete her degree and apply for full-time positions that she is qualified for. Sharmila needs to work on her understanding of customers and customer service skills. A customer service training course would be worth her time.

Recommendations: The report tells what actions might be taken in the future based on the data included in the report.

Supervisor's signature: *Elaine Wallace*

Employee's signature: *Sharmila Chowdhury*

Example: Meeting Minutes Report

Community Swimming Pool Board Meeting Minutes

August 9, 2001

President Donald Quincy called the monthly meeting to order at 7:10 P.M. on August 9 in the board room. Ray, Cathy, Mary, and Julie were absent.

TREASURER'S REPORT: Account balances as of July 31, 2001 are as follows:

> Operating Account: $30,456
>
> Capital Account: $23,567
>
> Reserve Account: $34,000

PRESIDENT'S REPORT: NONE

VICE-PRESIDENT'S REPORT: NONE

BUDGET AND FINANCE: NONE

HOUSE: Maggie met with the blind company and is getting estimates for new carpet for the banquet room. The new ice machine is working well.

GROUNDS: A new box for reservation sheets was installed for the tennis courts. New garbage cans with wheels are being priced.

POOL: A new diving board was installed.

MEMBERSHIP: Three new families were presented and accepted for membership.

ACTIVITES: The outdoor pool will close on September 3, with an end of summer party.

YOUTH: Bingo is set for this Saturday for children ages 7–10. The cost is $2.

SPORTS: Nadine requested a sign-up sheet for tennis teams for the fall.

COMMUNITY LIAISON: Linda reported that the garbage is not being picked up promptly in the alley behind the facility. Twice, garbage bags sat for an extra week before being picked up. She will call the city to address this problem.

OLD BUSINESS: A motion was made and passed to approve the rental of the facility to the Community Dad's Club on the third Tuesday of each month.

NEW BUSINESS: Don reported an incident with the lifeguards on July 4. Apparently, a group of teens insisted on putting up a volleyball net in the open pool rather than in the volleyball pool. When asked to abide by the rules, vulgar language was used. It was decided that in the future, lifeguards should call the pool manager to handle these situations. Anyone refusing to listen to the pool manager will be asked to leave the pool.

NEWSLETTER: The deadline is the 15th of each month. If you have any photos of the Fourth of July Parade that you would like to share in the newsletter, please give them to Carol as soon as possible. Label all photos with your name, address, and phone number, so she can return them to you.

The meeting was adjourned at 8:46 PM.

Intro-duction: The introduction can be brief for some reports.

Body: The body of this report is divided by headings.

Recommen-dations: This report includes the recommendations under each heading.

PRACTICE ▶

Check your answers against the answer key at the back of the book.

1. Write a report describing the progress you have made in this book so far.

_____

_____

_____

_____

_____

_____

_____

_____

_____

_____

_____

_____

_____

_____

_____

_____

_____

_____

_____

_____

_____

_____

_____

_____

_____

_____

_____

_____

_____

_____

_____

_____

_____

_____

_____

_____

_____

_____

_____

Appendix—Model Essays and Workplace Writing

▶ MODEL ESSAYS

The following are samples of different kinds of essays.

PERSUASIVE ESSAY SAMPLE

Question

Community members in Smithville are at odds about an Advanced Placement English Program in their schools. Should the district implement such a program and why?

Response

The Smithville Independent School District needs an Advanced Placement English Program for several reasons. First, though the schools have been doing fine in the past without an Advanced Placement program, neighboring school districts and private schools are introducing similarly advanced English programs in their high school curricula. Smithville graduates will be competing nationally for admission into some of the finest universities. For the students capable of completing an Advanced Placement English Program, the school district has an obligation to offer the program, as well as a reputation to uphold at home for former graduates and taxpayers.

Since other schools are beginning to offer and advertise these advanced courses, it will soon be important for Smithville to have them available too, for without them the district could lose many fine students—students who will be nationally recognized under other school's names otherwise. Many years ago schools did not offer algebra classes either; however, today most colleges and universities begin at the calculus level in math, well ahead of the typical algebra student. Just as schools have had to progressively take on more specialized classes in mathematics, so will they need to provide more advanced English instruction in order to prepare students for their future and keep up with the changing face of education.

Though not all students will be in the program, most will benefit from it anyway. Just as it would be unjust to ignore less advanced students, it is similarly unjust to ignore the more advanced students in our schools. Regular classes are crowded and often fail to engage the minds of both categories of students. The Advanced Placement English Program, however, could eliminate some of the pressure on regular level teachers to "reach" all levels of students, allowing them to better meet the instructional needs of the average student. Offering an Advanced Placement Program would also improve the reputation of Smithville's schools—better meeting the needs of students and receiving more national acclaim in the long-run.

Smithville should introduce the Advanced Placement English Program as soon as possible in order to maintain the support and reputation the district has already won. Implementing the program now will also help those students who are currently competing nation-wide for admission into college. In addition, the project will alleviate the pressure on teachers to accommodate varied levels of students. Moreover, the schools offering more opportunities are, naturally, favored by parents and achieving students. Smithville Independent School District wants to be a preferred school district. Therefore, the district will need to implement an Advanced Placement English Program in the near future in order to fulfill its duties to parents, teachers, and students.

PERSUASIVE ESSAY SAMPLE

Question

We hear in the news all the time that American public schools are failing our students—American students are not competing favorably on international tests and schools seem to be faring worse all the time. Are our schools really doing worse today than in the past?

Response

American schools are doing a better job today than in the past. First, why don't American students do better on international tests? It's a fact that European and Asian countries, even war-torn and Third World countries, often do better than American high school students on math and science tests. How is this possible? When looking at the scores, we must examine who is taking the tests. In the early grades, a broad cross section of students in all countries are pretty much taking the tests. If you look at the scores, you'll see that the United States gets the top marks at this point. Starting in high school, however, the United States' scores plummet. It's also around high school that European and Asian schools have weeded out less-capable students from their education systems. However, American high schools include all students: those who are academically talented, those who don't speak English, those with disabilities, and so on. So the comparison is not fair. The international tests compare the most talented European and Asian students with a broad cross section of American students.

Even if we discount international comparisons, however, it sometimes seems as though schools are still doing a worse job today than they were in 1950. Is this true? No, it's not. Let's look first at domestic standardized test scores. In 1995, 75% more students scored above 650 on the SAT Math test than in 1941. If you factor out the Asian-American population, 57% of African-American, Hispanic, and white students did better on the SAT Math in 1995 than in 1941. The norms for the SAT Math test were the same between 1941 and 1995, so the higher scores are comparable. Test scores on the ACT college entrance exam have also increased each of the last three years.

Do test scores really mean that schools are doing a better job? Let's look at other indicators of success. First, students are learning more at school now than in the past. If you visit your local high school, you'll find that many students are taking college credit courses in high school. In fact, a high school student can begin college as a junior just based on coursework completed in high school. Today, students are expected to learn at least 50 more years of history than they were in 1950—and in the same amount of time. Major events have occurred during the last 50 years—including the Korean War, the Vietnam War, the fall of communism. Calculus used to be college math—now most high schools offer two years of calculus. DNA had not been discovered in 1950. Today, DNA, genetic engineering, and a host of other topics are standard fare in a first-year biology course—that's a course that typically includes a textbook with more than 50 chapters and 1,000 pages. In 1950, we classified all living things as either plants or animals; today, living things are classified into six different kingdoms, and some scientists are already postulating as many as eleven different kinds of life. On top of standard academics, students are also learning computer literacy and computer programming. Students are learning more academically today than ever before.

In addition, graduation rates are rising. In 1870, only about 3% of high school students graduated from high school. In 1995, 83% did, and 60% of those went on to college. So more students are graduating and going to college, too.

If public schools are doing so well, why are Americans unhappy with them? Americans feel that schools are doing a bad job because they aren't meeting the needs of their kids. But which needs are we talking about? That all depends on the child—and every child is different. The problem is there is no consensus on the criteria upon which our schools are to be judged. If a child is athletically inclined, a school should provide a strong athletic program and opportunities for that child to gain an athletic scholarship to college. Students with disabilities need special programs, too. In fact, every child requires something special, and so schools are left meeting too many needs.

This is not a new issue. Even in the 1950s and 1960s, newspapers were filled with articles complaining about the poor quality of American schools. In fact, our discontent stems from a conflict inherent in the American mentality. We are torn between our democratic principles of providing a free and appropriate education for everyone and achieving excellence. As Americans, we do not want to leave any child out—and so federal law mandates that all public schools must accept all students and meet their needs, including non-academic needs. Public schools provide breakfast and lunch for students, accommodations and self-sufficiency training for students with disabilities; public schools even bathe students and administer feeding tubes to those who can't eat. At the same time, we want the best for our children. Public schools are expected to provide special education, athletic, gifted and talented, vocational, music, and art programs, too, whereas our international competitors focus only on academics. We are not happy with our schools—even though they do so much more than those in other countries—because they are not perfect.

Schools are working harder and meeting more needs today than ever before. Our schools are doing a better job than they did in the past—even though it may sometimes seem otherwise. Will Rogers summed it up well: "The schools are not as good as they used to be—and they never were."

SAMPLE ESSAY FOR A SCHOLARSHIP APPLICATION

Because I have the skills and attitude to make a difference, State University should feel confident in investing in my future with a scholarship. For example, as President of the Russian Club, I increased enrollment 400% in one year and initiated many new programs (peer tutoring, an environmental clean-up, a borscht cook-off, and so on). The success of the Russian Club during my presidency earned it Best Club (out of 50+ clubs) at Home Town Community College; a distinction it had neither before nor since my leadership. Within four months at Local Telephone, Inc. and just out of high school, I received Employee of the Month and Most Valued Player awards. During my tenure at Progress, Inc., I climbed almost instantly into leadership roles, where I successfully led teams of my peers. My open-mindedness, willingness to take risks and take on challenges, and my leadership skills fueled these successes. These same qualities ensure my success at State University and beyond, making me a valuable resource for classmates and future State University graduates.

No matter what a job demands, I am willing to learn whatever is needed to succeed in that position. Unlike many of my peers in auto insurance, I entered the field with little knowledge of motor vehicles, repair techniques, or claims adjusting. And yet, I have advanced in this field very rapidly. Currently, I am the second-fastest adjuster in my office at Safe Auto Insurance (out of ~15). I credit my success, in part, to my ability to learn and apply new information quickly. I consistently completed training courses at the top of the class. I also sought out mentors, spent time before and after work asking questions, and practiced my auto adjusting skills.

Because of my willingness and ability to learn quickly, I will achieve my goals. My determination to learn, grow, and succeed at State University will empower me to do so. Moreover, I know from past experience that my can-do and helpful nature is contagious, and it will also help those around me at State University to succeed. State University can be a part of my future successes by awarding me a scholarship.

SAMPLE ESSAY FOR APPLICATION TO COLLEGE

Describe one of your most important accomplishments.

One of my most important accomplishments was my work in Russia. With the help of my husband, I was able to gain a basic knowledge of Russian culture, "survival" Russian, and a job lead before leaving for Russia. After arriving in Russia, I got a job as the first native speaker to teach English conversation at the Sokolniki campus of Moscow Linguistics University in Moscow, Russia. I worked for rubles—not dollars. I was responsible for teaching thirteen hours of evening classes to second-, third-, fourth-, and fifth-year students of English. I was also responsible for conducting a weekly seminar on American culture for the other teachers in the English Department. During the days, I worked on a textbook for Russian students of English, produced much-needed audio materials for the English Department, and took Russian courses at the University.

I consider my work in Russia a major accomplishment because I had to learn not only a new language, but also a new and substantially different, way of life—one of hardship and uncertainty in transitional Russia. I had no copy machines, textbooks, or heating available for my classes. I was left to my own imagination and ability to barter in producing activities and materials for my students. In my home life, I learned, among other tricks, to live without a refrigerator by hanging plastic bags with perishables out my window. Moreover, I quickly learned the way to get things done in Russia—how to find food, how to travel, how to get the paperwork that I needed to stay out of trouble with the authorities—and I made a contribution to the community to which I belonged.

SAMPLE LETTER TO THE EDITOR OF A PERIODICAL

Dear Editor:

Our daily news is often filled with reports of troubled youth in a violent world that we don't understand. However, here in our own community there is a group of young people who are setting a positive example and spreading peace and harmony. The concert presented by Jacksonville In Harmony, last Sunday, May 6th, brings hope to our community and serves as in inspiration to our country.

Talent and time were provided by this diverse group of young people. Their songs of praise rang through the beautiful setting at the newly constructed Fellowship Hall. To those in attendance, it was a time of inspiration and celebration. Please join me in recognizing Jacksonville In Harmony for their contribution to our community.

—Hope Daniel, Jacksonville In Harmony Mentor

▶ WORKPLACE WRITING SAMPLES

The following pages have samples of different kinds of workplace writing.

SAMPLE COVER LETTER

September 26, 2001

1234 Modella Drive
Little Rock, AR 45890

Ms. Joan Hamood
Campus Recruiter
XYZ Company
College Town, NY 10002

Dear Ms. Hamood:

I enjoyed speaking with you Friday at the Home Town Community College Career Fair. As I mentioned then, I would like to be considered for XYZ Company's internship this summer. I have two years of work experience, and I am currently pursuing an associate degree in Technology at Home Town Community College. My resume is attached.

Based on my research, I am convinced that I am a good match with XYZ Company. I am passionate about technology and I enjoy dealing with people and customers. As a customer service representative at Jones Repair Services, I was awarded Employee of the Month twice in one year out of thirty employees. In addition, I have maintained a B or better in all my technology courses at Home Town Community College. My ability to serve customers and my knowledge of technology are a good match for XYZ Company's needs.

I also have the strong time-management and teamwork skills you mentioned would be key to this position. During the last year, I have worked part-time while going to College Town Community College. Juggling both work and college has helped me refine my time-management skills and learn more efficient ways of getting things done. My grade point average has stayed above a 3.0 and I haven't been late to work once during this time. A good example of my teamwork skills is the role I played in the Community College's blood drive. Last spring, I worked with a team of four other students to set a blood drive goal, advertise the event, and recruit student volunteers. We exceeded our goal of pints donated by 10%.

Please review my attached resume. I think you will find that I am qualified to do a good job for XYZ Company this summer. In addition, I have the drive to work very hard. Please contact me at 432-555-7890, if you need more information. I look forward to talking with you about the internship. I will give you a call next week to set up a time to meet.

Sincerely,

Thomas Perez, Jr.

Thomas Perez, Jr.
Enclosure: Resume

SAMPLE COVER LETTER

May 4, 2000

3009 Palmeras Court
Hilton, FL 56894

Mr. Bill Jenks
Pflugerville Independent School District
1401 Pearson Drive
Pflugerville, TX 78660

Dear Mr. Jenks:

The Region XIII Education Service Center has recommended Pflugerville ISD as a school district participating in their 2000–2001 Alternative Certification Program (ACP). As a participant in ACP, I am seeking a teaching position in English as Second Language (ESL).

My commitment to working with students extends beyond my involvement in ACP. Over the past five years, I have been a teaching assistant, advisor, mentor, and tutor working with international students of all language backgrounds. I spent last summer tutoring adult immigrants in English and helping them prepare for the Citizenship Exam. While a student at State University, I taught English part-time to ten limited-English proficient children at the local elementary school. I enjoyed working these students and watching their progress in English. I would bring the same joy and patience to your school district as an ESL teacher this fall.

By sharing my enthusiasm and knowledge, I can make a worthwhile contribution to your school. If you have any questions about ACP or my training, please contact Martin Lukas ACP Coordinator. Please contact me if you have any questions about my background. I will call you next week to talk about setting up an interview.

Sincerely,

J. Francis Hunt

J. Francis Hunt

Enclosures: Application
               Resume
               Transcripts

SAMPLE RESUME

MELISSA R. RABIN
123 Cherry Blossom Drive
Palo Alto, CA 94304
(605) 555-7122, email: mrabin@email.net

EDUCATION

CALIFORNIA COMMUNITY COLLEGE, Palo Alto, CA
Associate Degree, Business Administration, May 1999

EXPERIENCE

JOHNSON INSURANCE, Palo Alto, CA   1999–present
Administrative Assistant
- Maintained all files for an insurance agency
- Created and set up a new filing system used by three departments in the agency
- Trained five other staff members on word processing software

MACY'S, Palo Alto, CA   1997–1999
Sales Associate
- Sold clothing to customers and monitored inventory
- Exceeded monthly sales quotas by 12%

MCI, Palo Alto, CA   Summer 1996
- Verified customer accounts and answered questions

HOPE SOUP KITCHEN, Palo Alto, CA   Summer 1996
Project Manager
- Stocked the food pantry, prepared and served hot meals to families, and cleaned up the kitchen and the dining hall two days per week

SPECIAL SKILLS AND AWARDS
- Fluent in Spanish
- Proficient in the use of Macintosh and IBM-compatible computers; familiar with MS Office
- Most Valuable Team Player Award, MCI (July 1996)

SAMPLE RESUME

JOSEPH P. DANIEL, JR.

3216 Pegasus Drive, Orem, UT 90229

(803) 555-8383, email: daniel@email.net

WORK EXPERIENCE

SAFE AUTO INSURANCE, Orem, UT   1999–present

Claims Team Leader

- Supervised a team of 5–8 field adjusters by evaluating each adjuster in person and monitoring their work product
- Increased team expertise by mentoring new adjusters, training them on new estimating software and wireless technology, and conducting quarterly skills certification exams which were correlated with pay raises and bonuses
- Improved team response time by assigning tasks based on adjusters' strengths, stocking vehicles, and reducing drive times

NEWTOWN INSURANCE, Orem, UT   1995–1999

Claims Adjuster

- Settled home and auto claims by inspecting property damage and negotiated settlements with customers and vendors
- Reduced costs by repairing rather than replacing property, minimized reinspections, and collaborated with multiple suppliers

JONES INSURANCE AGENCY, Orem, UT   1994–1995

Customer Service Representative

- Answered customers' questions about their auto insurance policies

BOOKS FOR PEOPLE WITH VISUAL IMPAIRMENT, Orem, UT   1993–1994

Project Manager

- Produced audio recording of a 700-page, 2nd-year Russian textbook by recruiting and training volunteers, securing the use of equipment, and organizing the workflow

HONORS AND AWARDS

- Good Job Award, Books for People with Visual Impairment (September 1994)
- President, University Russian Club 1993–1994
- Dean's List 1993–1994

EDUCATION

UNIVERSITY OF UTAH, Orem, Utah

Bachelor of Arts, Russian/Slavic Studies, May 1994

Proficient in Russian and French

SAMPLE ESSAY ON A JOB APPLICATION

What goals have you set for yourself that you want to reach in the next five years? Ten years?

Within the next five years, I would like to be able to integrate my experience in insurance with my public relations and computer skills. Presently, I see management and training as two fields where my combination of skills would be valuable. Since 2000, I have been taking business and computer classes at Home Town Community College. Within the next ten years, I would like to use the knowledge and credits that I have been accumulating into a four-year university degree. A university degree would help me advance and contribute to higher-level functions at work.

SAMPLE BUSINESS LETTER

October 14, 2001

Sumita Patel
2345 Main Street
Jacksonville, MO 64829

City Utilities
700 West Fruth Street
Jacksonville, MO 64829
Re: Account no. 211558378612

Dear City Utilities:

I am writing this letter of complaint after enduring almost two months of frustration with your services. I have attempted friendly and sympathetic negotiations with several representatives of your company (most helpful were Sam and Joyce). However, I have reached a limit to my patience and tolerance because of the way the situation has been handled.

I will first outline a brief chronology of the events that led up to this complaint. On August 23, my housemate and I moved into 2345 Main Street. On the same day, I notified City Utilities of our residence and opened an account in my name. The same day, a representative of your company threatened to turn off our utility services. We were told over the phone that a deposit of $130.00 should be received in your office by August 28. The following day, another representative came by and again threatened to turn off our utilities. We explained that our deposit was not due until August 28; nevertheless, he urged us to go directly to your main office and pay it in person. Again, I telephoned and was assured that our account was fine. I mailed the check for $130.00 that very day, in the names of both me and my housemate. A week later, a threatening representative returned to our door with orders to shut off our utilities. I hastily contacted your company again by phone and was notified that our account was in good standing. Yet our water was turned off the followed day and it took all of Friday afternoon and evening to get it turned back on. Sam assured me the problems had been resolved. However, the next week brought us the same sort of threats. Finally, Joyce spent quite a bit of time untangling the problems, explaining that we had been hooked up to the wrong address.

In the course of these frustrating events, we received two outrageously expensive bills and were assured by both Sam and Joyce that they indeed were not ours to pay—so we did not. At the same time, Joyce explained that the documentation of our deposit of $130.00 had been lost (although Sam had confirmed it previously). Joyce said that if we sent her a copy of the processed check, she would return the deposit to us as compensation for our hassles. We requested this document from the bank, wrote a letter of explanation, and sent it to Joyce's attention. We have repeated this action three times—but Joyce has yet to receive the documentation.

What I would like for you to do about this situation is not unreasonable. My requests follow:

1. Upon presentation, in person, of the requested documentation of our original $130.00 deposit, I would like a full refund.

2. I would like an investigation of our account to ensure that our account number does indeed correspond with our address and the meters read for our bills.

3. I would like for you to check for leaks in the plumbing system external to our home to see if water is leaking.

Thank you for your time and prompt attention to this matter. I trust you will rectify these problems as soon as possible.

Sincerely,

Sumita Patel

Sumita Patel

City Utilities
700 West Fruth Street
Jacksonville, MO 64829
(216) 471-7789

June 2, 2002

Sumita Patel
2345 Main Street
Jacksonville, MO 64829

Re: Account no. 211558378612

Dear Ms. Patel:

This letter will serve to confirm our telephone conversation of June 2, 2002, wherein I advised you that City Utilities has decided not to hold you liable for the outstanding balance for the above referenced account. I further advised you that City Utilities has dismissed any claim it has against you concerning said account and will recall your file from the credit agency to which it has been inadvertently sent.

Sincerely,

Carmen Hernandez

Carmen Hernandez
Attorney for City Utilities

cc: Credit Collections
        P.O. Box 347
        Killeen, TX 76540
cc: Mitchell Jaekle, Attorney-at-law

SAMPLE BUSINESS LETTER

American Mortgage Company
P.O. Box 19876, Minneapolis, MN 55440

1-800-555-3467

January 22, 2002

Sumita Patel

2345 Main Street

Jacksonville, MO 64829

Dear Ms. Patel:

Thank you for taking the time to speak with me about your recent experience with American Mortgage Company. You mentioned a number of errors that occurred during the processing of your mortgage loan. It is our intention to provide a worry-free process to our customers. I assure you that the service you received is not typical of what we provide. Please accept my apology for the problems.

Now that your loan has gone through, you will be working with our servicing office personnel. They are located in Frederick, Maryland and can be reached at 1-800-555-3467. Your loan reference number is 57430238. I am confident that you will be pleased with the service.

Again, thank you for your comments and for choosing American Mortgage Company for your loan. We will be working hard over the life of your loan and hope you will be pleased with our service in the future. We value your business and want to keep it.

Sincerely,

Tim Walton

Tim Walton

Customer Service Representative

SAMPLE BUSINESS LETTER

FANCY CHIPS

1003 FRANKFORD AVENUE / JACKSONVILLE, TX 75766

PHONE: 548-222-8904 / FAX: 548-282-7004

WEBSITE: WWW.FANCYCHIPS.COM

March 29, 2002

Jean-Luc Bibaud
24 Main Street
New Summerville, MA 02821

Dear Mr. Bibaud:

Thank you for your recent letter about the black substance you found in a package of Fancy Potato Chips. We have analyzed the substance you provided and determined that it is simply a piece of charred potato. I apologize for any inconvenience this may have caused you.

We take a lot of pride in the quality of our chips and make every effort to keep charred pieces of potatoes from being packaged with our Fancy Chips products. In fact, we filter the oil used to fry the potatoes and clean our equipment regularly. We also carry out visual inspections of our chips before they are packaged. Although we take these measures, sometimes a piece of burned potato will make its way into a package of our Fancy Potato Chips.

Please accept my apology for the unpleasant experience you had with Fancy Potato Chips. I am enclosing coupons for two free packages of Fancy Potato Chips and hope that you will find these packages exceed your expectations. Please do not hesitate to contact me again if you have any other problems or concerns about our products.

Regards,

LaToya Jones

LaToya Jones
Customer Service Representative

Publish Yourself! Inc.

P.O. Box 783, Jasper, ND 34902

Phone: 819-345-8923   Fax: 819-348-7834

Website: www.publishyourselfnow!com

April 9, 2001

Meinrad Meister
2894 Snow White Drive
Mansfield, FL 69821

Dear Mr. Meister:

I am an editor at Publish Yourself! In reviewing your recent manuscript, I have found three figures that are a part of another publication by your colleague Dr. Johnson.

We cannot reprint figures that have been previously published elsewhere without a letter of permission from the copyright holder. Although I recognize that Dr. Johnson is an acquaintance of yours, we still need a letter of permission before we can proceed. Generally, the copyright is held by the publisher of the publication rather than the author. If Dr. Johnson does indeed hold the copyright, then we simply need a letter from the publisher stating this along with a letter from Dr. Johnson giving us permission to use his figures in your book.

I am sending you a sample letter that you can use to request permission to use these figures. Usually if a request is written on the author's letterhead, the publisher responds more quickly. So you might request that Dr. Johnson assist you in this task. I am also attaching a copy of our copyright policy.

I look forward to receiving your letters of permission so that we can continue work on your book. If you have any questions, please contact me directly at the following number: 819-345-8923.

Yours truly,

Manny Jimenez

Manny Jimenez
Permissions Editor

Enclosures: Request for Permission to Reprint Form
　　　　　　Publish Yourself! Copyright Policy

SAMPLE MEMO

STATE UNIVERSITY
Brooklyn 🏛 Long Island 🏛 Westchester

MEMORANDUM

To: All students, faculty, and staff

From: Facilities Management

Date: May 23, 2000

Re: Holiday Schedule

The following hours will be in effect for the Memorial Day holiday.

SATURDAY, MAY 27, 2000

Rogers Hall & Dibner Bldg.   9 A.M. to 9 P.M.

Student Center   CLOSED

SUNDAY, MAY 28, 2000

Rogers Hall & Dibner Bldg.   9 A.M. to 9 P.M.

Student Center   CLOSED

MONDAY, MAY 29, 2000

Rogers Hall & Dibner Bldg.   9 A.M. to 9 P.M.

Student Center   CLOSED

PLEASE BE ADVISED—THE LIBRARY WILL BE CLOSED.

ALL FACULTY, STAFF, AND STUDENTS ARE REQUIRED TO HAVE VALID I.D. CARDS TO OBTAIN ENTRY TO THE BUILDINGS AND **MUST** SIGN IN AND OUT AT THE SECURITY DESKS.

Please follow safety guidelines at all times.

Thank you.

SAMPLE MEMO

MEMO

To: All Second- and Third-Shift Personnel
From: Kendall Chisolm, Third-Shift Coordinator   *KC*
Date: September 23, 2000
Re: Run/Walk for Children's Hospital

Time is money—and your time could mean money that's desperately needed for important medical research and services. I'm writing to ask for your time. As you may know, I volunteer at the Children's Hospital. Next month, the hospital is sponsoring a 5K run/walk. Will you participate? We need runners and walkers as well as volunteers to cover registration and T-shirt distribution. The run/walk will be held on Sunday, September 17. It starts at 9:00 A.M. If you'd like to help, please call me at extension 2120. The registration deadline is April 20. Please help us help children in our community. Thanks!

SAMPLE MEMO

Publish Yourself! Inc.

P.O. Box 783, Jasper, ND 34902

Phone: 819-555-8923   Fax: 819-555-7834

Website: www.publishyourselfnow!com

MEMO

To: All Personnel

From: Karl Stuart, Permissions Editor   *KS*

Date: January 23, 2002

Re: New Copyright Procedures

In order to better comply with the copyright law, we will start taking the following steps IMMEDIATELY.

1. *Copyright transfer.* From now on our copyright release form should read as follows:

   I affirm that I have written permission to use any previously copyrighted material included in _[insert title of the book]_ and that such documentation will be forwarded to Publish Yourself! Inc.

   I hereby assign and transfer ownership of [_insert title of the book_] (including the rights of reproduction, derivation, distribution, sale, and display), as protected by the laws of the United States and foreign countries. These exclusive rights will become the property of Publish Yourself! Inc. from the date of acceptance for publication. I understand that Publish Yourself! Inc., as copyright owner, has the sole authority to grant permission to reprint any parts of the book. (Please consult Carol should you wish to alter this wording in any way.)

2. *Contracts.* We are adding a new clause to all author contracts. This clause will state that it is the author's responsibility to obtain any necessary permissions. It may also state that the book cannot be published by Publish Yourself! Inc. without this documentation.

3. *Staff credits.* Please remove the names of all editors and layout managers from the inside front cover of all books going to the printer.

4. *Authors.* We will begin (gently) informing our authors of our policies as soon as the second letter goes out to them. We will also need to start following up on our requests for copyright from the authors. As a later resort, we may even offer to request permissions ourselves.

5. *Printer.* If the letters of permission have not been received by the dates that we are ready to send the book to the printer, then we will have to remove all previously published figures and tables for which we still do not have permission to reprint. (Of course, Don may have exceptions to make to this rule, such as continuing to wait for the permissions or trying to obtain them quickly via fax.)

Copyright infringement is very serious. We all need to work together to encourage authors to obtain letters of permission and to ensure that everything is accounted for in the authors' files. These problems can cost Publish Yourself! Inc. a lot of money.

Thank you for your cooperation.

SAMPLE MEMO

To: Our Volunteers
From: Fran Harris, Volunteer Coordinator   *FH*
Date: July 23, 2002
Re: Ten-Year Anniversary

Yes, we have had ten years of Neighborhood Volunteers in our community! As we celebrate the birth of an organization, we look to those who have been responsible for its growth. At first, I had planned to begin by recognizing those individuals who gathered one spring day in 1991 to form an organization that would pool resources and eliminate duplication of services. These people were the "founding members" of Neighborhood Volunteers, Inc. Though my intentions were good, and the records are well preserved, this would lead to mentioning every individual who played a major role in the process of Neighborhood Volunteers' growth over the last ten years. That list would be the size of the current local phone book, so instead, I will simply acknowledge the "founding members" (and you know who you are), with a simple word of gratitude to each and every one. I would, of course be remiss to not mention the three people who gave more time, effort, and financial support through the years. To the late Raymond Teague, and his beautiful wife Eloise, we are eternally grateful for sharing your dream of helping the less fortunate. Thank you also to Rev. Harold Lansford for giving us leadership and guidance to fulfill their dreams. The legacy of these people lives on and keeps growing. Their dreams and guidance have inspired the people of our community to create an organization that has developed 23 programs—each striving to meet the needs of our disadvantaged neighbors.

Our goals and purpose have always been directed to improve the quality of life in our community. People in this community have made each program successful, through volunteer efforts and financial support. The Raymond and Eloise Teague Center was built and exists because of these efforts. Just take a look at some of the programs that are highlighted in our anniversary newsletter, as well as some of our other literature. We've come a long way in ten years. Neighborhood Volunteers has provided services to thousands of people through our programs:

- energy assistance program
- transportation vouchers for medical appointments information and referral services
- community clean-up campaigns
- feeding the hungry through the soup kitchen and Manna Pantry
- childcare quality programs
- fire victim emergency assistance
- healthcare information and referral services which includes the very successful Prescription Application Assistance Program

- after-school programs
- teen driving safety awareness campaign
- student character value program

All of these services are a result of a need that was not being met previously in our area. None could have been created and become successful without the support of all the wonderful volunteers who have given their time and money to these efforts.

To you, the supporters, thank you for ten wonderful years and together, we will work to give many more years of Neighborhood Volunteers to our community.

SAMPLE E-MAIL MESSAGE

Date: Tue 09 May 2000 15:43:14 –0500
From: Ashruf Ishak <aishak@designcompany.com>
To: Beth Tidwell <b_tidwell@xyzcompany.com>

Subject: Photo Captions for Website

Hi Beth:

I hope your meeting last week went well. I made several content changes to the website last week and am working with Jackie Devo, our artist, to add the new graphic pieces to the website this week. However, before she and I go too far with the photos, we were wondering if you could help us by writing some simple captions.

Please go to http://www.yourwebsite.com/photos. There you will find the photos Jason and I selected for inclusion in your website. As soon as you have a chance, please review each photo and see if you can come up with a brief caption that we can use. You can e-mail me the captions, but please be sure to attach the photo number to each caption.

OK, that's all for now. Talk to you soon!

Ashruf Ishak
Designer
Design Company, Inc.
55 5th Avenue
Orion, CT 06001
Phone: 860-555-2384
Fax: 860-555-2790
E-mail: aishak@designcompany.com
Website: http://www.designcompany.com

SAMPLE E-MAIL MESSAGE

Date: Mon, 1 Oct 2001 12:33:24 –0500
From: Sara Chang <schang@xyzcompany.com>
To: All Employees <group@xyzcompany.com>
Subject: New carpet installation this weekend

ATTENTION

We will be getting new carpet installed in our office on Saturday, October 6. To help with the carpet installation, you are asked to do the following things by FRIDAY, OCTOBER 5, at 5 PM.

1. Please remove all your belongings and non-furniture items from the carpet in your work area.

2. Please remove everything from the surfaces of the furniture in your work area.

If you have any questions or need help complying with these requests, please call me at extension 555. Thanks for your cooperation!

Sara

Sara Chang
Ext. 555
Schang@xyzcompany.com

SAMPLE STATUS REPORT

STATUS REPORT

For the week of 11/13/99–11/20/99

Submitted by: Robert Evans

Department: Facilities

Completed:
- Repaired the damage to the roof from the weekend's ice storm. (This took a full two days.)
- Replaced the pipes under the sink in the men's restroom.
- Repaired the cracks in the wall in the 2nd floor Conference Room.
- Replaced light bulbs in the hallways.

In Progress:
- Painting the cafeteria

To Do (ranked by priority):
- Install the new window blinds, which arrived yesterday, in the 3rd floor Conference Room.
- Clean up the branches and other debris from the ice storm.
- Continue painting the cafeteria. I had hoped to complete this task by the end of the week, but clean-up from the ice storm took priority. I will probably not finish until the end of next week.

SAMPLE STATUS REPORT

SUMMER TRAINING STATUS REPORT
For the week ending July 27, 2001
Submitted by: Don Garza

On 7/27/01 I assisted you in the staff-development activities for special education teachers. We discussed the following items in this staff development:

- Overview of the upcoming audit
- Student tracking
- Documentation procedures

All staff present were told that it is highly likely that they will be interviewed by the auditing team. I hope that each person will take the information they learned in the staff development back to their campus and share it with their principal, special education staff not present, and the general education teachers.

Our next staff development seminar is scheduled for 8/7/01. We plan to discuss the modification requirements for general education teachers.

As always, I seek your input and comments on the planned training activities.

SAMPLE PERFORMANCE APPRAISAL

XYZ Company

Performance Appraisal

Employee Name: Sharmila Chowdhury

Employee Social Security No.: 333-33-3333

Employee Title: Summer Intern

Supervisor's Name and Title: Elaine Wallace, Director of Customer Support

Period covered: May 15, 2001 through August 15, 2001

I. Summary of performance

Sharmila was very efficient this summer in gathering and compiling data from our other offices. The data she compiled is valuable for our Global Customer Support Project and will be used to better meet our customers' needs in the near future. Sharmila communicated professionally and followed up promptly with all regional and local contacts. She worked tirelessly to get all the information needed. Using the data she had collected, Sharmila was able to begin a preliminary draft of recommendations for the future.

II. Characteristics of Effective Performance

Please check the rating and provide comments/examples where relevant.

< > **Exceeds Expectations (EE)**—check this rating when the employee has consistently exceeded your expectations in the area being rated.

<X> **Meets Expectations (ME)**—check this rating when the employee has achieved your expectations in most areas.

< > **Does Not Meet Expectations (DNME)**—check this rating when the employee's job performance in the area being rated is unacceptably low.

Leadership skills Sharmila demonstrated leadership in her ability to put together a contact list and use it effectively to gather the information needed for her project.	ME
Communication skills Sharmila communicated effectively with other offices as she acquired all the data needed in such a short amount of time.	ME
Initiative Sharmila showed initiative when she began an analysis and a preliminary draft of future recommendations for using the data she had collected.	ME
Teamwork skills Sharmila did a very good job of working with our other offices and administrative staff this summer. Her ability to get along with others and to convince others to work showed true team spirit.	EE
Time-management skills Sharmila was able to manage her time well. She accomplished more on this project over the summer than our office had been able to accomplish in the six months preceding her internship. She met all the deadlines.	EE

Recommendations for the future: Sharmila's performance this summer shows promise. If she is interested in becoming a permanent employee at XYZ Company, I recommend that she complete her degree and apply for full-time positions for which she is qualified. Sharmila needs to work on her understanding of customers and customer service skills. A customer service training course would be worth her time.

Supervisor's signature: *Elaine Wallace*

Employee's signature: *Sharmila Chowdhury*

SAMPLE REPORT INTRODUCTION

H.O.P.E. (Helping Others Pursue Enrichment), Inc. is in the business of helping people. Our organization is a non-profit social service agency that has been providing helping programs to our underserved neighbors in Cherokee County for the past ten years. It has always been our mission to identify gaps in services and to work with others in our community to meet these needs. Twenty-three programs have been developed in our decade of service by networking with local and regional agencies. The enclosed attachments will give further detail about our programs. Our multi-purpose H.O.P.E. Center is unique to this rural area. It sets an example to the nation for a one-stop shopping for human resource services.

We have successfully created programs through the efforts of a small staff (recently increased to 7 people), and a very frugal budget. Over the last ten years, we have increased our annual budget from $12,000 to $50,000. In comparison to other agencies, both local, state, and federal, this is an exceptional accomplishment.

The H.O.P.E. Center has a strong presence in our community; however, we are in need of funding for our Helping Children Program. This past year, the Helping Children Program served 1,200 children living in poverty in our county by providing food, clothing, school supplies, and other types of support. Although the program currently serves a large number of children, 500 others will go without our help this year. As our budget stretches to help these children, their numbers are expected to grow 15% in the next year. As the attached report shows, a grant of $3,000 would allow us to serve the needs of these children next year. Please consider supporting this program with your funding.

The support of the Children's Foundation would enable us to increase this valuable service and further our efforts to improve the quality of life for all citizens in our community.

Respectfully submitted by:

Helen Nguyen

Helen Nguyen
Executive Director

Answers

LESSON 1

1.

SUBJECT	DIRECTIONS
The vectors involved in the transmission of rabies from dogs to humans	Identify
Three ways to prevent the spread of rabies	Describe

2.

SUBJECT	DIRECTIONS
The implications of the argument that behaving ethically makes good business sense	Discuss
This argument to the behavior of companies today	Relate

3.

SUBJECT	DIRECTIONS
Western European culture with the Islamic culture during the Middle Ages	Compare
Each culture's scientific accomplishments, literature, and concepts of law and justice	Include information about

4.

SUBJECT	DIRECTIONS
The reasons that the U. S. government decided to build a canal across the Isthmus of Panama	Review

5.

SUBJECT	DIRECTIONS
Four factors that affect the rate of photosynthesis	Identify
The effect of each factor on the rate of photosynthesis	Explain

6.

SUBJECT	DIRECTIONS
Your goals in life	List or identify
How you plan to reach your goals	Explain

7.

SUBJECT	DIRECTIONS
The three main tasks of marketing	Identify

8.

SUBJECT	DIRECTIONS
The representation of courage in *Henry V* and in *The Charge of the Light Brigade*	Contrast

9.

SUBJECT	DIRECTIONS
Economic imperialism and political imperialism	Contrast

10.

SUBJECT	DIRECTIONS
The foreign policy objectives of Italy, Germany, and Japan in the 1930s	Identify
How each nation achieved its objectives	Explain

LESSON 2

1. Answers will depend on the topic and writer.
2. a. You could ask others for ideas about problems that concern them, listen to the news or read periodicals. A clip file would be a good source for this assignment.
    b. You could go to a local museum or art gallery or browse through art books in your local library. You could also use pictures on the walls of your home or buildings at your work or school for this assignment.
    c. You could browse your scrapbooks, photo albums, and resume for ideas. You might also write in your journal about your own areas of expertise and interests and your goals and dreams. What have you done to move toward your personal goals? What types of things are you proud of? What about you makes your friends and family proud of you?
3. Answers will vary from person to person. One possibility is shown here.
    a. The causes of teenage pregnancy or the options for a pregnant teen
    b. How to keep your computer virus free
4. a. The audience will be a college admissions committee. They will be looking for insight into your personality, goals, and values, as well as evidence that you can communicate effectively and logically in writing.
    b. The newspaper staff, and ultimately, the readership of the newspaper will be your audience. The newspaper staff will be more likely to print a letter that is engaging, interesting, easy-to-follow, and that makes points relevant to past material printed in the paper or to the general readership of the paper.
    c. Your biology teacher will be the audience of this essay. Your biology teacher will be looking for evidence that you have learned the content covered in the question.
    d. Your college composition teacher will be the audience for the research paper. He or she will be looking for a clear thesis, coherent topic, and evidence that you have used appropriate resources to research your topic. Your teacher will also be interested in your organization of the topics, writing style, grammar, spelling, presentation of sources, and your ability to follow the style guide or instructions provided in the writing assignment.
5. Answers will vary from person to person and depend on the piece of writing chosen.

LESSON 3

1. Answers will vary from person to person. One possibility is shown here.

    The Internet

    Scary

    Powerful

    Useful

    Over-touted

    Does it really save time? Or waste time like TV?

    So many connections

    New kinds of viruses, security, safety, privacy issues

    New kinds of businesses

    New ways of working—from home, in isolated areas, etc.

2. Answers will vary from person to person. One response is shown below.

I remember my first day in first grade. I sat beside my cousin John. It was scary. We were in an outside temporary building. The teacher was very nice—Mrs. Bracken or something like that. Her room smelled like crayons and she had a lot of stuff on the walls. The chairs were just the right size for us. There was a boy crying and his face was all red. My mom kissed me good-bye and waved. I stayed near my cousin all day and felt safe with him there. Then they told us our room and teacher were just temporary. Later, they reassigned me and John and I guess all the kids in our class to teachers inside the school building. Then John and I weren't in the same class anymore. I didn't like my new teacher and felt less secure for a long time after this happened. I guess it really affected me since I still remember it so well . . .

3. Answers will vary from person to person. One response is shown below.

What are genetically engineered foods?

Why should they be labeled?

Who will be affected?

Why wouldn't manufacturers want to provide this information?

When would it start?

Why would we want to know?

How would it be done?

What if they aren't labeled? What could happen?

Who will standardize the labels and claims and regulate their use?

Who eats these foods? Avoids them?

4.

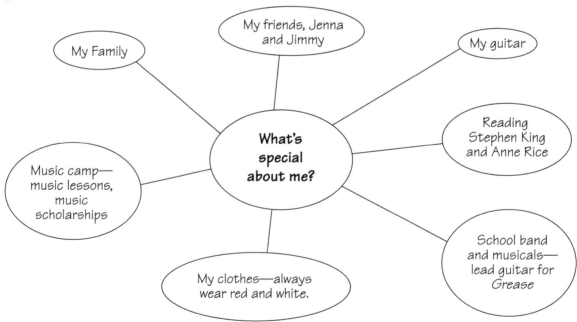

5. Answers will vary from person to person. See answers to 1–4 for examples.

LESSON 4

1. Building a prison near my home would benefit my community.
2. Uniforms are not a good idea for public schools because they suppress student expression and lower self-esteem.
3. Getting separated from my parents at the World's Fair was a terrifying experience, but it taught me that I could be self-reliant and that many people are available for help if you ask them.
4. If I were President for one day, I would focus on two issues important to me: reducing poverty and improving public education in the United States.
5. Answers will vary from person to person. See any of the examples of graphic organizers in Lessons 2 or 3.
6. Answers will vary from person to person. One response is shown below.

    Thesis statement: Teenagers get pregnant for a number of reasons.

    I.   Too much exposure to sexual material
        A.   TV
        B.   Movies
        C.   Advertisements
        D.   Rock music
    II. Unmet needs
        A.   Parents aren't giving enough attention
        B.   Need to fill an emptiness
    III. Wanting to grow up
        A.   Need for more responsibilities
        B.   Need for independence
        C.   Need for more attention
    IV. False information
        A.   From friends
        B.   From parents
    V.   Peer pressure
        A.   From friends
        B.   From self

7. Answers will vary from person to person and depend on the outline produced.

LESSON 5

1. Answers will vary from person to person. One example is shown below.

    Thesis statement: Building a prison near my home would benefit my community.

    Topic sentence 1: A new prison near my home would provide needed jobs and counteract the flow of people from our small town.

    Topic sentence 2: Building a prison in my community would stimulate our local economy and benefit local businesses.

2. Answers will vary from person to person. One example is shown below.

Thesis statement: Building a prison near my home would benefit my community.

A new prison near my home would provide needed jobs and counteract the flow of people from our small town. A prison would require construction, security, administrative support, cafeteria workers, sanitation, and many other services. People in my community could fill these positions. Every person in my community who finds a local job will have a reason to stay here.

LESSON 6

1. Answers will vary from person to person. One example is shown below.

Thesis statement: I would not recommend Boris Pasternak's novel *Dr. Zhivago.*

Supporting reasons:
  a. Too many characters
  b. Too many difficult names to keep up with
  c. Too many complicated subplots to try to follow
  d. Too many unimportant details
  e. Too many digressions—I lost interest
  f. Too many extraordinary coincidences—I didn't find it credible

2. Answers will vary from person to person. One example is shown below.

Although it's considered a great novel, Boris Pasternak's *Dr. Zhivago* is not an enjoyable read. The book is filled with an overabundance of characters, each possessing a polysyllabic Russian name that is difficult to pronounce, recognize, and distinguish from the next. The story is a labyrinth of subplots, which are easily confused with one another and difficult to follow. Pasternak provides entirely too many details of trivial importance that have no bearing on the main plot of the novel. He digresses often and advances to the end of the story so slowly that I eventually lost interest altogether. Even if I had been able to stay interested in the plot, the number of extraordinary coincidences that Pasternak expects the reader to digest would have turned me off. Despite its reputation, *Dr. Zhivago* was a major disappointment. If you are interested in this story, I suggest renting the movie instead.

LESSON 7

1. Answers will depend on the pieces of writing chosen by each person.
2. a. The writer begins with a startling claim and quotation, both of which get the reader's attention. However, readers who already have a strong opinion about Creationism or evolution may not be convinced or may be turned off.
  b. In fact, evolution and Creation can be combined and accepted as one general explanation of mankind's origin. These two explanations are not in conflict with one another, but actually need one another in order to complete the answer to mankind's questions.
  c. Answers will vary from person to person.
3. Answers will vary from person to person. See the examples in Lesson 7.
4. Answers will depend on the pieces of writing chosen by each person.
5. Answers will vary from person to person and depend on the thesis statement chosen. Examples of effective conclusions can be found in Lesson 7.

LESSON 8

1. a. The introduction is clear and well written, but it does not prepare the reader for the rest of the essay.

    b. I expected the last sentence to be the thesis statement, but these lessons are not discussed directly in the essay.

    c. Not really. They do not discuss the lessons learned on the trip abroad.

    d. No, they discuss other accomplishments.

    e. There are some specific examples, but they don't relate to the thesis statement.

    f. The conclusion does seem to stem from the information in the body paragraphs, but it doesn't really match the introduction to the paper.

    g. Answers will vary. Perhaps a new thesis statement and introduction should be written. Based on the revised thesis statement, the support in the body paragraphs and the conclusion can be made more directly relevant to the introduction.

2. Answers will vary from person to person.

LESSON 9

1. a. Yes. There are two main things that I really dislike about myself.

    b. Two things the writer doesn't like about himself

    c. Although some of the examples could be more specific, all of the sentences relate to the paragraph's main idea.

2. Answers will vary from person to person.

3. a. They are arranged spatially—room by room.

    b. This is an effective way to arrange the items because it's a logical way to think about an apartment.

    c. Yes, the sentence, "If you plan to clean your apartment once in a while, you'll also need cleaning supplies specific for each room," doesn't follow the spatial organization and breaks up the flow of the room-to-room listing. It should either be deleted or moved to the end of this paragraph or to another paragraph.

4. Answers will vary from person to person.

5. Answers will vary from person to person.

LESSON 10

1. you're
2. quiet
3. past
4. complements
5. desert
6. its
7. capitol
8. already
9. waste
10. principal
11. Whose
12. weak

13. site

14. write

15. There

16. wear

17. Answers will vary from person to person. One way to correct each problem is shown below.

    a. Look at the facilities in other countries, and you'll see the U.S. has far better facilities.

    b. Contributing time, money, and effort, John got the project off the ground.

    c. My father isn't sick—he's as healthy as a horse.

    d. I stayed up all night working on my paper.

    e. Employees must be prepared and on time.

18. Answers will vary from person to person. One way to rewrite the paragraph is shown below.

    A person who is interested in becoming a teacher—a profession that is in great need of talented people—should investigate the elements required to be a good teacher before making a final decision. On first thought, it might seem that a good teacher is one who is very knowledgeable of the subject matter: a master of what he or she wants to teach. However, others would disagree. Good teachers are those who connect with students and are able to interest students in the process of thinking and inquiring about the subject matter. Teaching is more than knowing the subject matter. It's understanding where students are and dreaming about where they can go with the subject matter.

19. Answers will vary from person to person. One way to rewrite the paragraph is shown below.

    Several months ago, February 29, I had just watched the ending of a very funny movie. I reached over, turned off the TV, and was just beginning to dream quite pleasantly when the familiar ring of my telephone suddenly startled me awake. Groggily, I answered my telephone. It was my best friend telling me he had just been given extra tickets to the Yankees game. He excitedly asked, "Would you like to go?"

20. Fewer; than

21. emigrated

22. invented

23. accepted

24. inferred

25. adapt

26. affect

27. badly

28. lay

29. lying

30. Set

LESSON 11

    1. Answers will vary from person to person. One way to rewrite the paragraph is shown below.

        What a person accomplishes in life depends on what he thinks he can accomplish. Self-esteem is a good indicator of one's future. Low self-esteem can cripple a person. Although he might be qualified to accomplish a particular project, he will probably fail because he will give up more readily.

LESSON 12

1. Answers will vary from person to person. One way to rewrite the paragraph is shown below.

    Last Sunday Henri Henklebeck, my best friend, called. "Did you hear that the circus is coming to town?" he asked. After a long discussion about the circus, we decided to spend the afternoon there and hung up.

2. Answers will vary from person to person. One example for each type of figurative language is shown below.

    a. The dog was a rocket zipping across the field.

    b. The dog zipped across the field like a rocket.

    c. As we left for the last time, our old home sighed a good-bye.

    d. The dog was covered with a billion fleas.

    e. On the day of the test, I woke up late to a thundering bolt of lightning. I knew it was going to be a good day.

LESSON 13.

1. a. Define the ADA. Identify who is covered. Identify who is not covered.

    b. Explain what the term *disability* means in the ADA. Give examples of who does and does not qualify as a person with a disability.

    c. Describe some aims of the ADA. List or describe the processes covered by the ADA.

2. Answers will vary from person to person and depend on the essay question selected. One response is shown below.

    Aims

    ■ Protect people with disabilities from discrimination

    ■ Increase wages for people w/ disabilities

    ■ Increase employment rate for these people

    Covered processes

    ■ Applications

    ■ Hiring/firing

    ■ Promotions

    ■ Salary/benefits

    ■ Training

3. Answers will vary from person to person and depend on the essay question selected. One response is shown below.

    a. The ADA, or the Americans with Disabilities Act, is a federal law intended to prevent discrimination against people with disabilities.

    b. In the ADA, the term *disability* refers to people who meet specific criteria.

    c. The ADA aims to protect people with disabilities from discrimination.

LESSON 14

1. Answers will vary from person to person and depend on the exploratory strategy selected. One response is shown below.

   Aspects of mountain climbing
   - physical training and conditioning
   - planning a route
   - climbing locations
   - weather requirements
   - climbing tools and equipment
   - provisions needed

2. Answers will vary from person to person and depend on the topic selected. A response for the topic of mountain climbing tools and equipment is shown below.
   - What types of tools and equipment are needed for mountain climbing?
   - What types of safety equipment are available?
   - Where can you find the equipment?
   - What's the bare minimum one would need to begin mountain climbing?
   - How expensive is the equipment?

3. Answers will vary from person to person and depend on the topic selected. To find information about the topic of mountain climbing tools and equipment, you might check the following sources.
   - encyclopedia
   - climbing how-to books
   - climbing-related magazines
   - survival guides
   - travel books
   - Internet sites
   - first-hand accounts from mountaineers (memoirs, biographies, autobiographies)

LESSON 16

1. Answers will vary from person to person. Refer to Lesson 3 for examples of prewriting strategies in action.

2. Answers will vary from person to person. One response is shown below.
   RECORDING FOR THE BLIND, Austin, TX   1993–1994
   Project Manager
   Produced audio recording of a 700-page, 2nd-year Russian textbook for blind students by recruiting and training volunteers, securing the use of equipment, and organizing the workflow; completed project one month ahead of schedule

3. Answers will vary from person to person. See the examples in Lesson 15 and in the appendix at the end of this book.

4. a. As Administrative Assistant at Taiwan Foods International, I wrote all outgoing correspondence and spoke with customers on the phone.

b. As Student Representative, I listened to student ideas and took them to monthly meetings. I was able to persuade the university administration to keep the library open an extra hour each night during final exams.

c. As part of the college's Green Team, I worked with ten other students to keep the creek that runs through campus free of litter and other types of pollutants.

d. When I was a tutor at the Learning Skills Center, I helped students overcome math anxiety by helping them cope with their fears. Not only did I help them study for upcoming math tests, but I also helped them become familiar with other aspects of the testing situation, such as the room and the format of the test.

5. Answers will vary from person to person. See the examples in Lesson 15 and in the appendix at the end of this book.

LESSON 17

1. Answers will vary from person to person and depend on the letters chosen.

2. Answers will vary from person to person. One response is shown below. Other examples are provided in Lesson 16 and in the Appendix.

January 22, 2002

Your company letterhead

Customer Service Department
Duplicating Parts Company
201 Kentucky Avenue
Iowa City, IA 67459

Dear Sir/Madam:

Our company recently ordered a replacement part (Part # A458) for our photocopying machine (Model # 5002). The part that we received, however, does not fit our machine—it appears to be for a different model of photocopier.

I am returning the incorrect part to you along with its packing slip. Please provide us with the correct part. I am also attaching a copy of our original order form.

I look forward to receiving the correct part. I appreciate your prompt attention to this matter. If you need any additional information, please do not hesitate to contact me.

Sincerely,

Your name
Your title

Enclosures: Photocopy part
              Copy of packing slip
              Copy of original order form

LESSON 18

1. Answers will vary from person to person. One response is shown below. Other examples are provided in Lesson 17 and in the Appendix.

> MEMO
>
> To: All Employees
>
> From: Jill Montgomery, Vice President Human Resources *JM*
>
> Date: November 15, 2002
>
> Subject: Open Enrollment for Medical and Dental Insurance
>
> Materials for this year's open enrollment are in! Please come to the Human Resources Department to pick up your packet. There are several changes in the Medical and Dental plans we will be offering next year. You'll need to make your selections by December 15. Plan changes will be effective January 1, 2003.

2. a. Yes, the message is short and to the point.

  b. The message is fairly clear, but the subject line is not meaningful.

  c. It's simple, but it's not effective. Uppercase letters are not used effectively. The information could have been listed or separated to make it easier to read. The writer could have been more polite.

  d. No, it seems fine.

3. Answers will vary from person to person. One response is shown below.

> Subject: New carpet installation this weekend
>
> Date: Mon, 1 Oct 2001 12:33:24 –0500
>
> From: Sara Change <schang@xyzcompany.com>
>
> To: All Employees <group@xyzcompany.com>
>
> We will be getting new carpet installed in our office on Saturday, October 6. To help with the carpet installation, you are asked to do the following things by FRIDAY, OCTOBER 5, at 5 PM.
>
> 1. Please remove all your belongings and non-furniture items from the carpet in your work area.
>
> 2. Please remove everything from the surfaces of the furniture in your work area.
>
> If you have any questions or need help complying with these requests, please call me at extension 555. Thanks for your cooperation!
>
> Sara

4. Answers will vary from person to person and depend on the e-mail message selected.

LESSON 18

1. Answers will vary from person to person. One response is shown below.

> **Progress Report**
>
> Submitted by: Joy Tan
>
> Date submitted: July 5, 2002
>
> This is a progress report for my work in *Better Writing Right Now.*
>
> ▪ I began this book on June 1.
>
> ▪ I completed Section I on June 5.
>
> ▪ I completed Section II on June 15.

- I completed Section III on June 20.
- I completed Section IV on June 25.
- I completed Lessons 15–18 on July 3.
- I will complete Lesson 19 today.
- I plan to browse the examples of writing in the Appendix over the next week.